MW00572114

NANNY'S ATTIC

NANNY'S ATTIC

You Want to Put That Thermometer Where?

Carolyn Goddard

Mountain Memories Books
Charleston, West Virginia

Mountain Memories Books
Charleston, WV

©2012 by Carolyn Goddard

All rights reserved. No part of this book may be reproduced in any form or in any means, electronic or mechanical, including photocopying, recording, or by any information storage and retrieval system, without permission in writing from the publisher.

First Edition

10 9 8 7 6 5 4 3 2 1

Printed in the United States of America

Library of Congress Control Number: 2012954656
ISBN-13: 978-0-938985-32-7
ISBN-10: 0-938985-32-9
Book & cover design: Mark S. Phillips

Distributed by:

West Virginia Book Company
1125 Central Avenue
Charleston, WV 25302
www.wvbookco.com

TABLE OF CONTENTS

ACKNOWLEDGMENTS

I wish to thank many people who have helped make this book a reality:

Family and friends who provided wonderful stories, inspiration and encouragement.

My husband, Fred, who looked at my stories and declared, "You have a book here." He set aside some short stories he had been working on, began editing and typing, and never looked back. Fred is nothing, if not stubborn. Those times when I might start to doubt, he believed and kept moving forward.

The many wonderful people we met in our travels, who would listen to my stories, tell one or two of their own, and tell us they wish they had written those memories down. This encouraged us to keep going and to stay with the book/journal format. Many said they felt our country was in need of some upbeat stories that showcased positive values.

Bill Abraham, Floy Hawkins and Kay Jeffers who provided valuable feedback on the early drafts.

Josh Mason, our illustrator.

Last, but certainly not least, Bill Clements, our editor at Mountain Memories, who took our wounded little pigeon of a manuscript and transformed it into an eagle.

Introduction

You are about to enter Nanny's Attic. Once inside, you will find the memories of an unwimpy grandmother, my collection of true stories that picture the spirit of a child. Many of the stories are humorous, some poignant and some just a little wacky. All will rekindle memories of your children, grandchildren and of your own childhood. If you are reading this, there's a good chance that you too are a grandparent. If, like me, your short-term memory and other aspects of your mental health have been damaged by your grandchildren, and some days you are not sure whether or not you are a grandparent, there are helpful clues.

- *You might be a grandparent if you think Black Eyed Peas are something you serve with ham.*
- *You might be a grandparent if your grocery bill is more than your house payment.*
- *You might be a grandparent if you think a ho is a garden tool.*
- *You might be a grandparent if you havent seen your cell phone in three days.*
- *You might be a grandparent if there is no food in your house, and there are ten pairs of flip-flops in your entry way.*
- *You might be a grandparent if you have ever actually mailed a letter.*
- *You might be a grandparent if you wear a wristwatch.*
- *You might be a grandparent if you have ever looked at an ugly baby picture and said, Isnt she beautiful!*
- *You might be a grandparent if two or more Little League umpires call you by Mr. or Mrs. and your last name.*
- *You might be a grandparent if you have ever driven five hundred miles to watch a five-year-old play a soccer game.*

Whether or not you are a grandparent, if none of our stories make you laugh or cry, you should take this book back to the store and ask for your money back. You may not get it, but at least you gave it your best shot. Life is for those who show up.

If the stories do make you laugh or cry, you clearly care about children. There are many children in the world who are worthy of our smiles and our tears. My pledge to you is that half of my profit from *Nanny's Attic* will go to a child-related charity. The Rotary Foundation will be a primary recipient of these funds because of their world-wide work that impacts child mortality and well-being. I will certainly also consider other qualified charities based on the relative number of written requests by readers.

To the Kids

These stories are dedicated to our grandchildren.

It is no accident that you are here. You are designed by our Heavenly Father and entrusted to your family for guidance and nurture until you are ready to step into whatever role you will serve in His world.

We have been blessed to watch, listen and record some of your early observations as you worked to make sense of your new world. Your insights, sometimes poignant, often humorous and sometimes a little scary, are a priceless treasure to us. When our own children – Rich, Craig and Beth were growing up, we were often too busy to record and write about those times in their lives, so we appreciate a second chance to include a few of those special moments here also.

You are descended from a long line of people who served God and overcame many difficulties to make a better life and to pass along those things of value they had learned. Most of your ancestors came from Switzerland, Germany, Russia, England and other countries in Europe. You have inherited their determination, imagination and intelligence to make of life whatever you desire. You live in a country where that is possible. It is now your turn to learn and pass along those things of value that you discover on your journey

These stories are about your start on that journey. Seeing the world through your eyes has refreshed us and renewed our appreciation of what a wonderful gift life is. Thank you!

Cast of Characters

(In order of arrival on the playground)

Grandma Pearl — *Fred's Mom* 1908 -1995

Nana Ruby — *My Mom* 1921- 2009

Fred — *Husband* 1941

Carolyn — *That's me* 1945

Rich — *Son* 1965

Craig — *Son* 1967

Beth — *Daughter* 1969

Aly — *Granddaughter* 1993

Hannah — *Granddaughter* 1995

Eric — *Grandson* 1996

Andrew — *Grandson* 1996

Zach — *Grandson* 1996

Jackson — *Grandson* 1999

Jacob — *Grandson* 2000

Eva — *Granddaughter* 2005

A host of friends and family of various ages — *Some aren't telling*

THE EARLY YEARS

Shut up and Eat Your Pancakes

My love of a bargain is legendary among family members. It's not that I have any objection to spending money. It's just that I like to know I get the best deal possible when I do it. Rich and Craig love to tell the story about their first trip out west. I believe they were too young to remember much, but they have heard Fred tell it and have adopted his version.

We were somewhere in Oklahoma on a sunny Sunday morning. Although we skipped going to church in the interest of travel time, I had Rich (4) and Craig (2) decked out in their red blazers, and we were looking for a good breakfast stop. A few miles from the motel, I spotted a diner displaying a large banner promoting a special, "PANCAKES $1.99."

We took a table among cowboys in their dress Stetsons and boots, and ladies in their Sunday finery. We ordered breakfast, and when the waitress asked what the children wanted, I said, "They'll have pancakes." Breakfast soon arrived and everyone dug in.

One of the well-dressed ladies at a nearby table looked with affection at the boys and said, "Isn't that sweet? Would you look at those children eating their pancakes like little gentlemen?" With that, Rich, self-appointed spokesman for the two, looked up, and I knew it was going to be trouble.

"Pancakes! We don't even like pancakes! We hate pancakes!" Then, pointing to me, "She made us eat pancakes!" The diner erupted in laughter. Rich, sensing an audience he could work with was about to continue when I shot him one of those *Wait 'til I get you back in the car* glances, and he thought better of it. By the time we did get back in the car and headed toward our destination, I was over the embarrassment, and I began to see the humor myself.

Little did I know at the time the incident was to become one of those classic family memories. To this day, unsolicited complaining by a family member is likely to be met with the response, "Shut up and eat your pancakes!"

What I Really Meant Was...

When our son, Rich was four, he was sitting at the top of the stairs leading from our living room to the sleeping area upstairs. He was happily playing his favorite game with his father. He would push a kid-size basketball gently off the top step, and it would bounce down the stairs to Fred at the bottom. Fred would toss the ball back up, and the cycle would be repeated.

The stairs were open on one side except for a wrought iron handrail. When the ball bounced off the side of the stairs for the third or fourth time, Rich blurted out, "Son of a B….!"

Fred reacted instinctively, and yelled, "What did you say?"

An equally startled Rich questioned softly, "Oh, little boys not supposed to say son of a B….? Just supposed to say son of a gun?"

Fred barely got out of the room in time to avoid letting his laughter be interpreted as approval. "Did you hear that," he asked? "Where do you suppose he got that?" We both had a short list of suspects, headed by a close family member, who shall go unidentified to protect the guilty.

Cool It Santa!

Our town provided an opportunity for small children to visit Santa. The visits were broadcast over a local cable channel. I decided to take the children for a visit. When Santa had Craig on his lap, he asked him if he went to school.

"I go to kindergarten," Craig replied.

"Kindergarten is a great place," said Santa! "You get to play and learn new things and make friends with other boys and girls."

"I don't like girls!"

"Of course you like girls," said Santa! "Girls are nice."

"I hate girls!" Craig was clearly agitated now. *Don't push it Santa*, I thought. Craig had learned a few inappropriate words, probably from his Grandpa. I was afraid he might express himself a little too forcefully if he was backed into a corner. I shuddered as I thought of the phone calls we might receive as a result. I breathed a sigh of relief as Santa got the message and quickly changed the subject.

Later, as a teenager, Craig would reverse his opinion of the opposite sex – so much so that we began worrying again about phone calls.

Beth Arrives

The possibility of Alyssa, Eric and Andrew began with the birth of our daughter Beth in 1969. Beth caused considerable excitement upon her arrival, especially on the part of her two older brothers, Rich and Craig. Four-year-old Rich was doing his duty spreading the word that I was in labor. He announced to the neighbors that my water tank had busted and I had to go to the hospital. Some 24 years later, it was our youngest, Beth, who would begin the next generation of our family.

We Knew It All Along

My life as a grandparent began December 28, 1992, the day Alyssa Louise arrived. I have since realized all of the grandparents in the world share this observation or its equivalent: "Isn't that the most wonderful, beautiful and brilliant piece of humanity you've ever seen?" You saw your own children that way when they were born, but with grandchildren your eyes become glazed over and you instantly know you'll spoil them rotten! Actually, when you study this new piece of creation that God has entrusted to your family, it is easy to overlook that he-or-she has some resemblance to a bald bowling ball, who screams, cries a lot and needs changed often because a rainbow is hovering over the crib. They do enter into our hearts and our world with great impact. Alyssa Louise was no exception. We watched her first moments in the nursery when she played with the monitor cords in her crib and tried to move her mouth in speech, and decided that we were witnessing a child prodigy.

True to our predictions, as we watched "Aly" grow in the months after her birth, we found that once she learned to talk she would amaze us with the things she would say.

Her first actual conversation with me occurred when she was twenty months old, as we were driving home one day "Nanny," she said, "Someday, I want to be a doctor."

Startled, I asked. "Why do you want to be a doctor?"– thinking that she would have no reply.

"Oh," she said, quickly, "So I can help babies"

Author's note: Fast forward sixteen years. As I am reading this manuscript prior to submission, Aly has just left for college. Her interest is in child psychology. I asked why she wanted to enter a field that requires a PHD as a working degree. "Eight years is a long time, Aly. Why child psychology?"

"Because I want to help children," was her reply. I was amazed at how close her thoughts were to the goal she announced at twenty months. It would seem that those studies asserting that our personalities are formed at an early age are pretty much on target.

Yellow Means...

An experience with a two-year-old backseat driver made me realize just how early small children learn and want to emulate our behavior. I was waiting for a traffic light to change when a small voice chirped from the car seat in the back, "Green means *Go*, Nanny!" *That's pretty good,* I thought.

"O.K. Aly, what does red mean?"

"Stop."

"And, what does yellow mean?"

"Speed up!"

Busted!

Freedom

Aly was three when she and I attended our local fair, Town and Country Days. She rode the kiddy rides, visited the animals at the livestock barns and sampled the cotton candy. We had a wonderful afternoon.

Later on, at the fair buffet, I was carrying our dinner trays and looking for an open spot at a table. A look came over Aly's face as though she had suddenly remembered something very important. Before I could put down the trays, she bolted out the door and sprinted through the fairgrounds at top speed with me behind her yelling, "Stop! Aly! Stop!" When I finally caught up with her, I demanded, "Why did you run away like that?"

"Nanny," she patiently explained, "Don't you understand? Sometimes I just have to take a run in the park."

There Goes the Neighborhood

When Aly was three she learned that her mother was expecting twins. She told everyone she met that she was going to have twin sisters. Aly was still happily looking forward to twin sisters some months later when the sonogram told a different story. I thought it would be good to prepare her for what was going to happen.

"Aly," I asked, "What if the twins are boys?"

Without hesitation she said, "We may have to kill them."

Her position hadn't softened much by the time the twins arrived. She was staying with Grandma Faye when the call came from Daddy at the hospital, announcing the birth of Eric and Andrew. Grandma Faye said, "Her little heart was broken. She cried for over an hour" After a few visits, she would smile at them and touch their little hands as she slowly became accustomed to having two new brothers.

The honeymoon didn't last long though. By the time they were a year old, Aly had mixed feelings about them. They often looked at her with love in their eyes and called her affectionately Mum-Mum. When she was in a good mood she would gaze back at them, pat them on their little heads and say "Aw Honey, you can call me Mum-Mum anytime you want to."

The words were rearranged quite differently when they would get into her things. She would place her hands on her hips and say rather harshly, "Don't you call me MUM-MUM! I'm not your MUM-MUM!" Then she would push their little walkers and they would go flying across the floor.

A Little Potty Humor

Eric, Andrew and Zach were all being potty trained at the same time. Fortunately, two sets of parents were involved. I'm not sure two were enough. The boys' minds are about twenty years ahead of their backsides at this point.

Zach's mom and dad decided to remove the diaper and go with underwear after reading some book on the subject. Results were somewhat less than ideal. Zach related proudly on the phone, "Nan, I went on the couch, the table, the floor and everywhere!" It was a bit reminiscent of our first-born bringing us his diaper and powder and lying down to await the service he had become accustomed to expect.

Time for a family meeting!

Andrew, who tends to be a perfectionist, took his potty training very seriously. He became very upset and cried when his aim failed and he missed the little pot. His mother assured him it was okay and encouraged him to try a little more carefully the next time. Andrew quickly brightened and explained to Eric, "It's okay. It was a simple navigational error."

Jackson is in preschool now. Soon after returning from school one day, he asked me to walk him down the hall to the bathroom at his house. I asked, "Did you learn anything new at school today, Jackson?"

"Sure, Nan," he replied earnestly, "They're teaching us how to aim."

I suppressed my laughter as I struggled to avoid visualizing the trial and error attempts that a hoard of preschool boys must go through before finally reaching their objective.

This story was passed along by a motherly baby sitter:

Little Kenny needed to go to the bathroom quickly. He was standing at the commode, struggling to get his pants unzipped and everything properly aimed. Fearing an embarrassing accident, the babysitter asked, "Would you like me to help you, Kenny?"

A concerned Kenny replied quickly, "I don't know. Do you have cold hands?"

A Rose is a Rose…

Aly loved to help me plant flowers or weed the flowerbed. I have many fond memories of her crouched down, exploring a new flower with her nose. One spring morning as we approached the flowerbed, she squealed excitedly, "Look Nanny! A dandelion! Isn't it beautiful? Those are very hard to find, you know."

I was struck by the truth of her observation. As adults we may see many dandelions, usually as we are applying a shot of herbicide. But it's almost impossible for us to find one, at least not the way a four-year-old can.

Pocahontas

I took Aly to every Disney movie ever made during her first years. We watched Snow White and the Seven Dwarfs, Cinderella, Esmeralda and a host of other characters cross the big screen to enthrall us. None of them really took Aly's heart the way the movie "Pocahontas" did.

Aly talked of nothing but going camping like Pocahontas. She was four and a half and ready to take on the great outdoors! Grandfather and I, of course, heard the call of the wild with her and packed up our gear for the adventure.

We set up our tent and put the boat in the water. We fished, fished and fished with little success. Thankfully the campground was near a restaurant and we had a fine fish dinner that evening. Aly had gathered firewood for a marshmallow roast after dinner. She spent all afternoon gathering sticks, pine needles and anything else burnable she could find. I watched and helped with delight and encouraged her by saying that's the way the Indians did it. Many marshmallows were burned at the stake that evening, by Aly and several other children from nearby campsites.

Everything went smoothly until bed time. "MOMMY!" She was so busy during the day that she had forgotten about her Mom. I was surprised she hadn't remembered sooner. This was her first overnight far away from home. Mommy was two hours away and we were too tired from our busy day to make the journey back. I also reminded her that she hadn't slept in a tent the way Pocahontas had. That didn't help too much. The tears still were coming down. It was then I remembered we had a TV with a DVD player in our van. One more Disney film did the trick. She was soon sleeping in her tent with renewed dreams of Pocahontas.

Flying High

Sitting in the backyard one summer day, Aly and I watched a jet streak high overhead.

"Where do you think that airplane is going, Nan? To the moon? Heaven?"

Knowing we are on the southern approach path to the airport, I said, "Probably Pittsburgh. Would you like to ride on a jet someday?"

She said, "Oh yes!"

"Where would you like to go?"

"Pittsburgh!" she said quickly.

I thought that was probably a better choice than the moon or Heaven for now.

Selma

Selma's father was an anesthesiologist. Her mother told her that Daddy's job was to put people to sleep at a hospital. One evening at the dinner table Selma asked, "Where's Daddy?" Her mother explained that Daddy was not there because he had to work late. "Oh my," she exclaimed, "It must take a long time to get them all into bed!"

HOME

In March, just before his second birthday, Andrew was admitted to the hospital with a bad throat infection. During his stay, he was hooked up to an IV and endured numerous shots, cold baths and examinations. When he was finally released and Beth carried him through the front door of their house, he smiled and offered a single-word comment, "HOME."

Eric immediately tried to feed him. It was the first time they had been apart and they had obviously missed each other. That night in their beds, they chattered for a long time before drifting off, apparently catching up on old times.

He May Mean IT.

The twins both developed strong wills from the start. When they went to bed or arose in the morning, they always wanted to do it on their own terms. I put Andrew to bed one night when he was about two. I did the usual prayers, hugs and a kiss and told him it was time to go to sleep. Eric had fallen asleep much earlier. Andrew rose up all puffed up and said, "NEVER-NEVER!"

David, their Dad, also found them hard to put down at night. They would often climb out of bed and wrestle or wander around the bedroom. He would put them back into bed and say sternly "Stay in bed, and I REALLY MEAN

IT!" One night he put them into bed and repeated his usual "Get into bed and stay there!" But he forgot to add the familiar reinforcement.

Eric right away, caught the lapse and looked at his dad and said "And you really mean it?"

David said, "Yes."

Eric then looked at his brother and said, "HE REALLY MEANS IT, ANDREW!"

The Watch

Zach's mom gave him one of her old watches to wear. A two-year-old's first watch quickly becomes his favorite watch, and he wore it everywhere. Returning home from a dinner out with his parents a few nights later, Zach was devastated to discover his watch was missing. A call to the restaurant was unsuccessful. No watch!

For the next few days Zach would cry each time he thought about his watch, which was the case at bed time the following Sunday. A search through the drawers in the house produced more tears each time he was shown a "new" old watch. Finally, about ten thirty, Dad packed him into the car and headed for a nearby drugstore that stayed open late. Finally a fine new watch with Pooh, Eeyore and Tigger was accepted.

Zach slept soundly until morning wearing his new favorite watch.

How's That Again?

When Eric and Andrew were two and a half, their vocabularies were expanding rapidly, a bit too rapidly at times. They were in their car seats, and we were headed for one more gourmet meal at Kentucky Fried Chicken. I heard Eric say brightly to Andrew, "It's time to say DAMN IT!"

"Eric! Don't you want to be a good boy and not say bad words?"

"Nope. Want to be a bad boy, and it's time to say DAMN IT!"

I think it's going to be a challenge.

You Want to Put That Where?

December began with the familiar hustle and bustle of preparing for

Christmas. I had asked Beth for Tuesdays off from watching the twins in order to have a little time for final shopping and wrapping. It was not to be. The boys both became ill and required pretty much constant care for a couple of weeks. They both had responded to shots of antibiotics and were feeling pretty good by Christmas Eve.

During Andrew's final checkup, I was with him in the doctor's examining room. From the waiting room, Fred could hear Andrew's firm opinion on rectal thermometers. "NO! NO! GET THAT SOOPID THINGY OUT OF HERE! TAKE IT AWAY! NOOO!"

Even at two years, Andrew had no problem expressing himself on issues that were near to his heart, or other parts of his anatomy for that matter. After several attempts at inserting the thermometer in his flailing little body, the nurse sacrificed accuracy and took the temperature under his arm. It was normal and we left the doctor's office with Andrew much calmer and me exhausted and looking forward to a little of the peace on earth that was promised to arrive within the next few days.

Brudders

The twins usually carry on a running conversation while they are playing together. I heard Andrew say to Eric, "Let's pretend we're brudders."

"We are brudders."

"Let's pretend we're daddy brudders."

"What's a daddy brudder?"

"I don't know. Let's just pretend."

Sisters

"You and your sister really look alike."

"Of course we do. We're diagonal twins, you know."

The Ghost of Christmas Presents

Children have a way of getting quickly to the essentials of a situation. Rich and Zach took a tour of their neighborhood two weeks before Christmas. Zach enjoyed all the lights and decorations. As they pulled into their own

driveway, Zach made a quick evaluation. "Gee Dad, we got nuthin!" Mom and Dad quickly abandoned their "Haven't had time" position and put up a tree and decorations, bringing a smile to one three-year-old.

Andrew the negotiator, at Christmas time: "Mom, maybe we should look over these presents before they are wrapped."

To a four-year-old, turnabout is fair play. Zach received a set of play dishes for Christmas. He prepared Rich a pretend meal and presented it to him.

"Here, Dad. Now you can try some of this food that you don't like!"

One Christmas we gave Jacob a little chair. Jacob had been delighted when he opened the package and found his very own chair. Naturally I was surprised two days later to find him visibly agitated and running from room to room crying, "Where's my stinking chair? I can't find my stinking chair!"

I thought: *I've never heard Jacob use that kind of language. He must really be upset, or maybe something that didn't smell good has been spilled on it and it really is a stinking chair.* I asked his mother, "Gina, why does Jacob call it his stinking chair?"

Gina laughed, "Oh! Jacob has a little trouble with his *T* sounds and sometimes they come out with an *S* attached to them." Only then did I remember the bold lettering on the chair back: **THINKING CHAIR**.

Back Off Jack!

Barber Jack loved to tease the twins by picking them up and swinging them. He would turn them upside down and threaten to cut off all of their hair. Usually the boys were amenable to this. But, one day Andrew obviously had enough.

Andrew drew himself up to whatever height a three-year-old could manage and exclaimed, "I don't like ya, Jack! The truth is the truth, and I have to tell you the truth. I just don't like ya!"

Jack was broken up by the confrontation, but it didn't dampen his enthusiasm for teasing very much.

The Cat's in the Bag

For years, we have spent Christmas Eve at my mother's house with an extended family of parents, siblings, children, nieces and nephews, and finally grandchildren. We eat dinner and open presents. Then, adults visit over cookies and punch while the children play with their new toys.

Christmas Eve, when the twins were three, the extended family also included Mother's very aloof Siamese cat, Melang, who showed no inclination to waste any of his nine lives on two three-year-old boys. Melang spent the evening under the bed. Adults were doing their cookie thing, and the children were playing in the hall leading to the bedrooms. We hadn't heard the twins chatter for a while and sent nephew, Curt, to check on them. Curt returned shaking his head and said, "Come with me. You have to see this."

We followed Curt to Mom's bedroom. When we opened the door and turned on the lights, we saw the twins lying prone on the floor. Andrew held a hairdryer. Eric, a couple of feet away, was holding a large paper grocery bag. A trail of cat food pellets ran from the bed to the space between the boys. I asked, "What's going on?"

"Now we have to start over," Eric complained. "A few more minutes and we would have had him. When the cat comes out to get the food, Andrew is going to turn on the hair dryer and blow the cat into the bag. Now we have to start over."

The cat was having none of this and lived to enjoy many more Christmas Eve celebrations securely under the bed.

Booty Call

The twins were always close, but early on they maintained their individual opinions on how and when things were to be done. Their next-door neighbor Veronica related a story. Veronica was relaxing on her patio and listening to her radio when she noticed four-year-old Eric dancing to the music.

She heard Andrew ask Eric, "Are you shaking your booty?"

"Yeah. Are you going to shake your booty?"

"No. Not now. Maybe later."

I'm Not Taking the Rap

To say being a grandmother of twins requires stamina is like saying a hockey goalie may, on occasion, need quick reflexes. When the twins were about three, Beth came home from work and found me asleep on the couch and Eric and Andrew wandering freely about the house. We quickly decided it was time to surrender and turn them over to daycare. I regained the ability to function normally almost immediately.

On a visit to daycare, I learned childcare can be a little stressful for the child, as well as the provider. I entered the room where the children are kept and found all the children asleep on their mats, except little Hannah who was wide awake and sitting quietly on her mat. I also saw no adults in the room. Mrs. Snyder had just stepped out of the room to get a box of tissues, but I didn't know that at the time, so I feared the worst. Near panic, I blurted out to Hannah, "Where's Mrs. Snyder?"

A startled Hannah's response was, "I don't know! What are you asking me for? I'm just a little kid!"

In That Case…

Zach picked over his dinner and asked to be excused from the table. Zach would do this from time to time, anxious to return to play. Rich told him he needed to eat some more before leaving the table.

"I'm not feeling very well, Dad."

Not completely buying the story, Rich suggested, "If you're sick, maybe you should go to bed and rest."

"Dad," Zach explained impatiently, "I'm just a little sick!"

Short Clips

Andrew: "Mom, do you remember the dream I had last night?"

Beth: "What dream Andrew?"

Andrew: "No, of course you don't. You weren't in it.

Fred, walking by grandson, Eric: "Hi Buddy."
Eric, without looking up from his video game, "Hi Grampy."

Eric worries about why he likes his grandfather so much.
"I can't understand it. He makes me mind and I still like him."

Four-year-old Andrew, in a Superman outfit: "Mom, It's a great day for flying!"

Four-year-old Eric burst through the back door giggling uncontrollably.
"That's the funniest thing I ever saw! Juliana just cut a worm in half, and it crawled away in both directions."

After a lengthy period of observation in the back yard, Eric announced to his mother, "It's a bug eat bug world."

Time Warp

I have never been a big believer in reincarnation, but Andrew's description, at four years of age, of his imaginary friend and family gave me pause. His favorite playmate, besides Eric, was Hey Heron. Hey Heron played baseball and had many impressive athletic achievements. Andrew would describe his adventures and talents in great detail.

In addition to having an imaginary friend, Andrew also states that he was married before and has five children. He names each of them and gives their ages and describes their physical appearance and personalities in detail.

Andrew also claims to be ten years old. I ask him how he can be ten in June when he was only four in April.

Andrew answers as though it should be obvious, "Because I ate my salami and cheese and vegetables."

The following day I asked Andrew how old he is, expecting to hear either four or ten years old. Instead he replies, "Twenty -five."

"Andrew," I asked, peering down into his little face, "Why do you want to be twenty- five?"

"Because when you a twenty- five, you can do anything you want to do."

Just Trying to Help

No matter how young we might be, there are always a few things that need to be corrected in our lives, and there is always someone who is more than willing to make those corrections.

Beth observed Eric chasing Andrew with a pair of pinking shears. Knowing four-year-olds and scissors are a bad combination, she grabbed the scissors first, then the child.

"Hey young man, where are you going so fast?"

"Oh Mom, I'm just going to snip off that hair that's standing up on the top of Andrew's head."

Too Bad

Rich, Melanie and four-year-old Zach were on the plane home from Tobago. Melanie had underestimated the tropical sun and was visibly suffering from a bad sunburn. She was in pain and her skin was peeling.

"Are you going to die, Mommy?" asked a concerned Zach.

"No, honey." Then, in need of a little sympathy, she added, "But what would you do if Mommy did die?"

"I guess I'd play a lot with Daddy,"

Jacuzzi Kitten

Beth had always wanted a fluffy kitten, and on Mother's Day, when the twins were four she got "Scratches" as a present. The kitten survived being chased and nearly trampled by the twins for about a month until they tired of the game.

Some days later, Andrew came up from the playroom in the basement and sounded the alarm. "Mom, come quick! Your Mother's Day present just fell in the Jacuzzi!" Fortunately, Scratches was never in any real danger. The Jacuzzi had been abandoned by the previous homeowner and was dry. Beth was able to lift Andrew into the Jacuzzi to rescue Scratches, who seemed to be enjoying her reprieve from the twins.

Mom 1 Britney 0

Eric suffered from a stomach virus all night and made repeated trips to the bathroom worshiping the white goddess to alleviate his distress. He was awake most of the night and finally said to his mom, "You aren't getting any sleep at all."

"That's o.k. Eric," replied Beth. "That's what Moms are for – when you are sick or have a problem. That's why God gives you a Mom to take care of you."

Eric smiled weakly through his distress. "You're a great Mom. If you were Britney Spears or Paris Hilton, I'll bet you wouldn't be here for me."

Bunny Hop

There is no doubt in my mind that Eric and Andrew visited planet earth in former times as hunters and warriors. Almost since they could walk, they have wielded plastic swords and spears. They have constructed homemade bows and arrows and a myriad of snares and traps to attempt to capture many of God's critters.

Driving home one day, as I near their house, I see Andrew stalking something. He is walking very slowly holding a plastic milk crate upside-down. As he sees me, he lifts a finger to his lips to request quiet. He lifts two fingers in the air and points across the street. I see two baby bunnies peacefully munching on some clover.

As Andrew crosses the street, he learns that bunnies are a lot quicker than a five-year -old with a plastic milk crate. The bunnies, however, seemed content to let him practice his stalking skills and would bounce just out of reach and continue grazing while awaiting his next attempt. Finally, Andrew gave up, but he was still smiling as he returned to his yard. I could tell he was already working on Plan B.

It Sucks!

Fred and I were working with a group making chocolate-covered Easter eggs for our church fundraiser. We broke for lunch and found ourselves across the table from Web, an enthusiastic four-year-old who was engaged in conversation with the lady seated beside him.

"I love vacuum cleaners! Do you have a vacuum cleaner?"

The lady replied, "Yes I do, Web."

"What kind is it?"

"I'm not sure what brand it is, but it has a big ball on the front."

"That would be a Dyson," Web declared confidently. He then continued matter-of-factly with some of the features of the Dyson vacuum cleaner.

Fred was impressed and commented to Web, "You really know a lot about vacuum cleaners."

"I love vacuum cleaners! I have my own Dirt Devil."

"Is it a good one?"

"It sucks!"

Barely able to contain himself, Fred commented, "That's a good thing. Right?"

"Yeah," Web replied proudly, "It really sucks!"

My Nanny

When Jackson was a baby, we didn't get to South Carolina to visit him often. Fred was in his last year on the job and involved with the physical and emotional demands required by the redesign and downsizing of the manufacturing facility where he had worked for the past thirty years. We saw Jackson maybe two or three times in his first year and he didn't have the chance to become familiar and comfortable with us during those early months.

On a visit when Jackson was two, I sat near him on the couch as we watched television. I explained to him that I was his other grandmother "Nanny". He gave me that look of uncertainty. He knew about his grandmother "Nanna Brymer," but he wasn't too sure about this stranger claiming to be his "Nanny." It didn't take long for him to warm up to me though. A day or two later, we were sitting on the same couch and his little fingers came across the couch and rested gently on my arm. It was a moment to remember. I was in! I was his Nanny.

Close Call

One afternoon, four-year-old Jackson and his two-year-old brother, Jacob, were playing with their toys in the family room. Their mother, Gina, came in and began to discuss the matter of naps. She asked, "Do you boys want to take a nap, or do you want to stay up?"

"We want to stay up, Mom," Jackson replied.

"Okay, but we plan to go to a restaurant this evening. If you get sleepy and cranky, you can't go. Can you be good if I let you stay up?"

"Yes, Mama," they replied in unison.

As soon as Gina left the room, Jackson said, "Wow, that was a close one Jake! We're okay. You can throw me the football now."

Otay Buckwheat

Jacob was nearly three and had shown almost no inclination to talk, beyond an isolated word now and then. When he wanted something, he would often grunt or gesture and his older brother would interpret for him. His parents became concerned and took him to a specialist. After examining him and running some tests, the doctor didn't find anything wrong. He felt Jacob would probably get around to talking in his own good time.

Fred's theory was that Jacob might not feel he had anything interesting to say, and he was perfectly willing to let his older brother, Jackson, do his talking for him. During our next visit, Fred sat down across the table from Jacob, and the drill started.

"Hey Jake," Fred began, "Say *O*."

No response.

Fred tried again. "Say *O*, Jake."

Jacob looked a little puzzled, but offered a soft, "O."

Fred continued, "Say *tay*, Jake."

Jacob responded, "Tay."

"Now say *Otay*."

Jacob was beginning to like the sound of this. With a grin, he replied, "Otay."

"Now say *Buck*, Jake."

"Bug."

"Close enough. Now say *wheat*, Jake."

"Wheat," Jacob replied.

Now say, "*Buckwheat*."

"Bugwheat."

"Now say *Otay, Buckwheat*, Jake."

Jacob was on a roll. "Otay, Buckwheat!"

Fred was delighted. Jacob had uttered a famous line from the *Little Rascals*, a delightful series about the adventures of a gang of neighborhood kids, which was very popular in the *'50s*. One of the kids, it might have been Spanky – I'm not sure, would offer the line as approval of whatever questionable scheme Buckwheat had just concocted.

I don't know if this was Jacobs first sentence, but he had the discovered the joy of speaking and would continue to offer, "Otay, Buckwheat," as a response to any suggestion or request from a family member. Jacob's vocabulary and verbal skills grew rapidly, and by the time he was three, he was able to hold his own with his peers on just about any topic. He may have held onto the "Otay Buckwheat" line a little too long, though. As we left at the end of our next visit, I told Jacob that we would see him in July at the beach, to which he replied, "Otay, Buckwheat!"

His mother overheard Jacob and quickly went about the task of reprogramming him to reply with. "Yes, Ma'am. No, Ma'am. That's a good idea, Grandmother," etc. Her efforts were highly successful and adding a little discipline to Jacob's manner of speech didn't dampen his enthusiasm at all. By the time Jacob was nine years old, he was a very polite third-grader who loved to talk with anyone of any age on just about any topic.

Nothing to It

During one of our annual Ocean City vacations, we had fished most of the day. The flounder were not very cooperative, but the croakers were unusually plentiful. Croakers are not as good to eat as flounder, but they are fun to catch. We caught several and threw most of them back. Three-year-old Jacob watched with no comment.

The next morning, as we left the dock, Jacob said, "I wanna fish."

His dad said, "Okay." When we got to a spot in the bay that had usually produced flounder, Fred cut the engine and started a drift. Craig baited up a rod, tied the handle securely to a cleat on the boat, and handed it to Jacob.

Fred asked, "What do you want to catch, Jake?"

"Cwoaker."

When Jacob's bait hit bottom, the rod tip dipped sharply. Jacob pulled back, and after considerable struggle, cranked up a nice croaker. Craig helped him swing it on board. When he unhooked the fish and put it in the ice chest for him, Jacob reeled in the last couple of feet of line, leaned the rod up against the side of the boat, and sat down.

Fred asked, "Do you want to fish some more, Jake?"

Jake replied, "Nope," leaned back in his seat and closed his eyes. Apparently, he had achieved his goal for the day by eight thirty and was ready for a nap.

Just Tan't

During our July trip to Ocean City, three-year-old Eva was sullenly picking at her breakfast. Her mother asked, "Why aren't you eating your grits, Eva?"

"I tan't. I want you to feed me."

"Sure you can. You know how to feed yourself, Eva. Just take your spoon and eat your grits."

Eva exploded, "I tan't! I want you to feed me now!" Gina was a bit taken back by the outburst and told Eva that she certainly would not help her eat unless she asked politely and said *please*.

"I tan't," wailed Eva. "I just tan't say please!"

Gina said, "Of course you can say please, Eva. You just said it."

"I just tan't! I just tan't say please!"

Needless to say, Eva went without her grits that morning. Worse yet, the whole family has adopted Eva's argument. When asked to do something they don't want to do, the reply is, "I tan't! I just tan't!"

In My Humble Opinion…

While visiting Eva for her fourth birthday, I slipped off my comfortable black Bass shoes. Eva entered the room, spotted the shoes and immediately exclaimed, "Those shoes are horrible!"

"Those are my shoes, Eva."

"They're still horrible."

I explained that I liked them because they were very comfortable and asked her if she knew what comfortable meant.

"Yes Nanny, but they're still horrible."

All of Eva's shoes sparkle and glitter and have lots of color. Perhaps we may have overdone the princess thing a bit with Eva. Either that, or at four years of age, comfort just isn't an issue with her. During our next visit, I learned Eva's observations and opinions were not limited to fashion.

"You know what Nanny?"

"No, what, Eva?"

"You eat more than my other Nanny."

Her other grandmother, Rosalind is fairly tall and slender. I tend to be a little on the round side, so I acknowledged, "Yes Eva, I probably do."

The expression on her face indicated she had not gotten everything she had hoped out of our conversation. A few minutes later – "Know what, Nanny?"

"No Eva, what"

"She doesn't pass gas either."

"That's nice Eva," was the safest response I could think of at the time.

When I told Nanna Rosalind the story, she said, "Oh, that dear child. It's good to hear that her capacity for pushing buttons and for exaggeration has not been diminished.

The Hazards of Snoring

Five-year-old Eva is dainty and looks the picture of a princess. Looks, however, can be deceiving. Eva has two older brothers, Jackson and Jacob, to deal with. To survive, she has developed the ability to take care of herself by hook or by crook. I will tell a bit about the hook part.

Eva always wants me to sleep with her when we are visiting. On the first night of our last visit, we had settled down to sleep after the traditional story reading. Following a good night's sleep, Eva informed me at breakfast, "Nan, you were snoring last night." I apologized and suggested she give me a little "sock" if I snored again the next night. That night she apparently took me at my word.

POW! – I woke with a punch on my arm that jolted me out of a sound sleep. I had no idea she could hit that hard. I told Eva, "That was quite a punch you gave me last night."

She said, "Nan, you told me to do it."

I said, "I know I did, but tonight could you just shake me a little?" She agreed and woke me gently a few times that night.

Critique

During our last visit with Craig and Gina's family, I baked an apple pie for the children to eat after we left. When we returned home, I called Eva and asked her if she liked the pie. She replied," I liked it very much, Nan. But you know if your grandmother makes you something, you are supposed to tell her you liked it, even if you didn't. You wouldn't want to hurt your grandmother's feelings."

"So did you really like the pie, Eva?"

"Well, I didn't eat the crust, but the filling was very good."

I've Been Robbed

It's hard to believe so much time has passed that Grandfather and I have also become Great Uncle Fred and Great Aunt Carolyn to six small ones. Four of them are my sister Mindy's grandchildren; Jacob, Ava, Erin and Herbie. Mindy died of cancer seventeen years ago at the age of thirty- six. On the way to the hospital two weeks before she died, I promised her I would always care for her children as long as I lived. They were seventeen, thirteen and eleven when she passed. God and Fred have helped me keep that promise, which now overflows to her grandchildren. I know Mindy is in a place God has prepared for those who must leave us, but I still often catch a glimpse of her in her daughter and grandchildren.

We joined her grandchildren, Erin and Herbie at their home to celebrate her third and his second birthday in March. The house was full of grandparents, great aunts and uncles, aunts and uncles, cousins and friends. There were mounds of toys and cards around the two celebrants. After they opened the toys, Erin turned to the first card. Apparently high expectations had been set. As she tore open the envelope and looked inside the card, a look of despair overcame her as she exclaimed, "What, no fifty dollars?" Everyone laughed. I believe Mindy, who was often outspoken would have appreciated Erin's direct approach to her problem.

Where are you going, Mama?

I will close this section with today's encounter with the Early Years.

Hayden, a T-Baller and junior daredevil, lives across the street. He and his best friend, Emmy, spend much of their time playing in the yard. Hayden is all boy and sometimes gets in trouble with his parents for overly adventuresome behavior.

Like all mischievous boys, Hayden can also touch your heart when you least expect it. Today, as his mother, Stacey was pulling out the drive in her car, she announced to Hayden, "I'll be right back."

Hayden's little voice rang out with, "Where are you going Mama? I love you Mama." There is no doubt in my mind that in that instant, Mama forgave every clean-up, broken lamp, tantrum and any offense ever committed during his adventures. I know I got a little teary. That flashback made me powerfully aware of how long it had been since I heard a small voice say, "I love you Mama."

I related this story to my 40 something daughter, Beth. With a grin, and in her best five-year-old voice, she said, "I love you Mama." I know she was messing with me for being overly sentimental. But, you know what? It still felt pretty good.

SCHOOL DAZE

Red Flags

"The reason I smell like smoke is…."
"Do we have insurance?"
"Mrs. Johnson really screams a lot."
"You won't believe what I can do on a skateboard."
"Can you identify an animal by its skeleton?"
"I'm tired. I think I'll just go to bed early."
"How much did that old vase in the hall cost?"
"My teacher hates me!"
"If I tell you something, promise me you won't yell at me."
"Nan, I need a mop real quick."
"All I did was….."
"Where do you keep that little fire extinguisher?"

Puppy Love

Alyssa was in pre-school and developed a great friendship with a little boy named Nicholas. Right before Christmas, Nicholas moved to Indiana. Aly was devastated. It was the first time a friend had left her. Before this, her friends had always been there.

One day she confided, "Nan, we played together every day – just he and I." The tears welled up once more. My heart ached for her too, watching as she learned the life lesson that it hurts when someone you care about is not there. Fortunately five-year-old hearts heal quickly, and in a few days she was back to her normal cheerful self.

The Call

By the time Aly was six we had spent many wonderful hours together. I know love must grow toward separation, and the time will come when she has her own circle of friends and priorities, but the relationship between a six-year-old girl and her grandmother is special. We are so important to our grandchildren when they are small. Aly left the following message on my answering machine. I copied it word-for-word.

"Hi Nanny…Would you like to come over to my house tomorrow?…

Today?....O.K.? This is Aly...Uh...I... It is fun over here at my house...so...I want you to come over.....'cause it's really fun...My brothers are having fun too. So...they're not spinning but they're kind of wrestling together. Well, I'm gonna say bye, and thanks for taking me to the merry-go-round and stuff at the park. So maybe you'd like to come over tomorrow....I love you....but...I love you so much! This is Aly....Remember, this is Aly. Bye!"

The sincerity of that broken little message still rings in my heart. I read it sometimes when I need a lift. Someday I hope Aly has a granddaughter who leaves her a similar message. Yes, the scriptures are correct. Love really is the greatest gift of all.

School Daze

One of Aly's second grade classmates was having some difficulty in one of her subjects and was spending some catch up time with her teacher. Aly realized her friend was forlorn about having to spend some special tutoring time.

Aly's attempt at encouragement was sympathetic, though maybe not fully uplifting.

"That's alright. You'll be out of there in about fifty weeks."

Aly: "Why do you call a person with $1,000,000,000 a billionaire, a person with $1,000,000 a millionaire, but a person with $1,000 just has a thousand dollars and no aire?"

Aly was looking through Grandfather's *Rotarian* magazine. She commented that a vegetarian and a Rotarian were a lot the same. I explained to her that they really weren't.

"Yes they are," she said. "They're both *arians*."

"Nan, I'm glad I'm not a girl."

"Why, Andrew?"

"Because I don't have to go through all that "Miracle of Birth" stuff."

Brenda, mother of two, after a hard day: "I'm beginning to understand why the mothers of some species eat their young."

Zach: "You never want to give a plant to my mother unless you want to see something terrible happen to it."

What Else Is Left?

One of the joys of being a grandparent is being able to share things that you enjoyed as a child. Six-year-old Aly is receptive to most of my suggestions. We were reading *Heidi* together, and we work and chatter together in the kitchen often.

We were icing Christmas cookies together. As Aly was spreading icing on a cookie, she said brightly, "Now I know how to ice cookies and we're almost finished with *Heidi*. I guess I know just about everything there is to know!"

Who, Me?

Aly received her first report card. We were happy to see that she got an "A" in each of her primary subjects. The comment section, however, was another matter. She received two grades of "S-." The comments were "Talking in class." "Listening and paying attention."

I asked, "Aly, what about these two grades of S-?"

"Oh Nan," she replied, "S- means almost superior."

Aly's "almost superior" grades followed her into the next year with a different teacher. Again the comment "Needs to work on controlling her talking in class."

Aly asked her mom, "Do you suppose those teachers just sit around the faculty lounge and say to each other, 'Aly talks too much'?"

Matter of fact, it's not a stretch to suspect that's exactly what happens - with ample justification.

Happy Birthday, Son.

Zach celebrated his fifth birthday with a cake and gifts at a party with his buddies. The next morning at breakfast, Rich poured him some milk in his favorite drinking cup. "Daaad," Zach complained, "I'm five-years-old! Don't you think it's about time I quit using THIS cup?" Rich agreed and replaced the sippy-cup with a more grownup version.

Can We Go?

When Aly was nine, we decided to take her on a trip to remember. Although we retained veto power, we allowed her some input in selecting the destination. Paris turned out to be Aly's top choice. She had seen a movie about the adventures in Paris of a little girl named Madeline. Paris was fine with us old folks. Her mom and husband, Mike, decided to come along too. We added a loop through the Black Forest to Innsbruck and on to Venice. A leg to Milan and up through Switzerland took us back to Paris. We had been scheduled to leave September 12, 2001. No one was flying out of Newark the day after 9/11. We delayed the trip for one year and left September 12, 2002.

There was a decided gap between Aly's tastes and those of the adults. She was delighted with the Eiffel Tower, Arc de Triumph and the boat ride on the Seine; not quite so much with Notre Dame and Sacre-Coeur, and even less with The Louvre. Ten-year-olds prefer to do their own paintings. Not surprisingly, we were poles apart on cuisine. "No Foie Gras or Cassoulet for me please!"

We had been told Parisians were curt and unfriendly. Not so. We found them to be kindly tolerant of a little girl with a McDonald's bag and four adults who needed a lot of help with the menu.

The golden arches worked equally well for Aly in Venice where the gondolas were okay, but the absolute highlight was the blanket of hungry pigeons in St. Mark's Square. She was able to find enough bread and cheese and wurst in the Alpine countries to survive and make it back to Paris, where

Fred and I put Aly and her mom and Mike on a plane headed for home. Then we headed south to the Dordogne to look at some cave paintings.

Encouraged by the success of that trip, we began planning trips for the other grandkids for when they turn ten. Andrew, Eric and Zach opted for Universal Studios and Key Largo. Jackson and Jacob went for a tour of the Wild West. We can hardly wait to see what Eva, the princess, selects. It's too soon to tell if these are unforgettable adventures for the grandchildren, but they work just fine for grandparents.

Sex Education

Aly came home from school beaming.

"Nan, I had the most exciting day at school!"

"That's great, Aly! What did you learn?"

"In science class, we observed two crayfish mating."

I'm thinking that's probably plenty of excitement for a group of fifth-graders, but the experiment was apparently not over.

"The next step is to separate them and see which one has babies."

Ozzie Likes Hamsters.

Beth and Mike have five children between them. They decided, enough is enough, and opted for an enthusiastic West Highland Terrier named Ozzie as the next addition to the family. Ozzie was especially enthusiastic when he was in the same room with the boys' hamsters.

Andrew was delighted. "Look, Nanny! Ozzie likes our hamsters."

"You misunderstand, Andrew," I cautioned. "He likes them for lunch. You should never take your hamster out of the cage when Ozzie is in the same room. Westies were bred to catch rodents. When Ozzie sees a hamster, he sees lunch."

"No, Nanny. Ozzie would never eat my hamster." He just couldn't believe this lovable little dog could be capable of hamstercide. This theory would soon be tested.

Six grandchildren, including Ozzie, were assembled in Andrew's room observing a demonstration of how tame Bam Bam, Eric's hamster, had become.

Andrew had the hamster in his hand and was petting him. In a serious lapse of judgment, Bam Bam leaped from Andrew's hand and hit the floor. Ozzie one-hopped Bam Bam like a shortstop going for a double play, and inhaled him.

The crew was frozen in horror, except for Jesse, who grabbed Ozzie and was about to attempt a Heimlich maneuver. The Westie opened his mouth to protest this rude interruption of his meal, and out popped Bam Bam, lying soggy and motionless on the floor. The crew was sure he was dead. Finally Aly got up enough nerve to prod him a little to see if he was still breathing. *Yep. He's still alive*. Hannah ran to get a towel and dried and fluffed him up a little. Bam Bam looked a bit stunned, but otherwise no worse for the wear.

Andrew, always the scientist, proudly announced the results of this unintended experiment. "Gee, Nan was right! Westies do eat hamsters after all!"

Is It Over Yet?

It was a few days after Christmas, and the last minute shopping, Christmas programs and church services, marathon meals, gift opening sessions and holiday visits were over. All the out of town guests had returned to their homes. Aly was spending the night with us. Beth had brought her by and stayed long enough to tuck her into bed. Her memory of a song played earlier in the week triggered a question in Aly's mind.

"Mom, how come we don't have twelve days of Christmas?"

Beth laughed, "Because we'd be broke, Aly."

Fred, in his recliner, still recovering from Christmas Past, mumbled, "No, we'd be dead."

Too Bad

Hannah, who joined our family with Beth's second marriage, has always been a gentle, unassuming, well-mannered little girl. As we learned at dinner one evening, she too has her limits. The grandchildren were discussing the day's school activities, with Hannah giving the first report.

"There's a boy in my class who is very sick with chicken pox."

Wanting to be supportive I said, "That's too bad, Hannah. I bet you feel really bad for him."

"Not really," she beamed. "He sits behind me and always pulls my hair and treats me mean. What goes around comes around, I always say."

Trading Up

Andrew was really upset. I had given Eric a pencil, and Andrew decided that it was the very pencil he wanted. Eric was unwilling to surrender the pencil, and I let him keep it.

Andrew was in a snit. He repeated over and over, "No fair! I want a new family! I want a new family!"

"Maybe that's not such a good idea," I cautioned. "You might get a family that wouldn't love you or feed you." Andrew was unimpressed.

"You don't understand, Nan! I want a new family, not a stupid family!"

There Are Rules.

Eric had realized that his mother and father were divorced. David, his father didn't live at his house. Mike, who was kind of like his father, but was called his stepfather, did live at Eric's house. It was all understandably confusing to a six-year-old. Beth patiently tried to explain, in terms that Eric might understand, what happens when a couple marries, divorces and remarries. When she had finished, she asked Eric if he understood, and he said that he did.

Two weeks later, Eric was on the porch playing with his step-sister, Hannah and her new friend. Eric asked his mother if Hannah's new friend had just moved there. "No, Honey," she replied. "Her mother is dating a guy up the street."

Eric looked shocked. "You're dating a guy up the street?"

"No, Eric," she replied. "The little girl's mother is dating a guy up the street."

"Oh yeah," said a relieved Eric. "That's right. You are only allowed to have two husbands."

The Fly Swatter of Justice

We grew up with the adage, "Spare the rod and spoil the child," but we used corporal punishment sparingly. It was usually reserved for behavior that would endanger the child or others, such as running into the street, or pushing your brother into the street. Blatant defiance, however, could also get you a pop on the backside.

I know that's all outdated and decried by psychologists, and we no longer have a rod or we can't find it. Most likely as our children got older, one of them hid it and we never bothered to find another. I do, however, keep a fly swatter handy for those days when normal methods of getting Eric and Andrew's attention fail. Anyone who has spent all day with a couple of energetic boys knows it's largely a matter of self-defense. It may even be illegal, but I say, "Go ahead. Put me in jail. I can use the rest!" Also, if the arresting officer has to spend a few hours with them, I figure he's going to be back trying to buy the fly swatter from me.

The twins made it clear that they understand the system. As I pulled the weapon from its resting place on a high shelf, Eric yelled, "Run for it Andrew! She's bringing out the Fly Swatter of Justice!"

Linda

For many years, Fred, his brother Dave and our sons Rich and Craig have taken a fishing trip over an extended Memorial Day weekend. They fish the bay behind Ocean City, Maryland for flounder or in the inlet for bluefish or sea trout. When Zach was six, his father, Rich, decided to take him along.

On about day three, the guys were drifting with the tide and waiting for a flounder bite. Zach asked his great uncle Dave if he had a wife, and Dave replied that he did.

"What's her name?" Zach asked.

"Linda."

"Linda? I had a babysitter once named Linda! Boy was she mean! She beat my butt something awful and said, 'You little Sh--!'"

As the boat erupted in laughter, the expression that had flashed across Rich's face made it clear this was the first time he had heard this story. He recovered quickly and continued fishing, making a mental note to ask Zach at the appropriate time, what sort of behavior might have provoked such a response by this babysitter.

The Seat of Learning

We had the children for a week while Beth and new husband, Mike, went to Cozumel for their honeymoon. The first night someone apparently pushed a button which transformed them into imps. They were laughing and bouncing off the walls, and every attempt at correction was duly ignored. Trying to transfer their energy to something more productive, I said, "Boys, get your book bags and do your homework." But there was more *Ignore Grandma and drive her up a wall.* It worked! After attempt number four, I applied the Flyswatter of Justice to their backsides and sat them on chairs to do their homework.

Eric protested, "I don't understand it. You used to be such a nice Nan! What happened?"

I know what happened. Switching to the role of parent again is what happened. It's much easier to be a good Nan than to be a Mom. My own children explain it to the twins, using an old Bill Cosby line. "Your Nan's still nice! She's old and trying to get into heaven now. You should have known her when I was a kid!"

Oh My!

As a favor to Rich, his neighbor Ellen picked Zach up at day care a few days before Christmas. Ellen's two-year-old daughter Alana was with them. Out of the blue, Zach declared daringly to Ellen, "I know a bad word!"

Ellen replied, "Zach, I would rather you didn't say any bad words in front of Alana."

"I'm going to," Zach replied. "It's sex!"

Ellen was a bit puzzled. "That's not a bad word, Zach."

Zach replied, "Ellen, I said sex, not six!"

Ellen just kept driving.

Cheap Date

Coming home from school, Andrew announced, "I bought myself a girlfriend today. It cost me five bucks!"

Stalling for time to come up with an appropriate response, I said, "That's nice." Still needing more time, I asked, "How did that happen?"

"I asked a girl if she wanted to be my girlfriend, and she said, 'I can't tell you until tomorrow.'"

Andrew, who has the patience of a falling tree, continued. "I asked her if I gave her five dollars, would she let me know today." Apparently the girl took the five dollars and became his girlfriend. I worried about this on several levels, but decided if five dollars is the most he spends foolishly on a girl, that's probably a cheap lesson.

Ow!

Zach and Rich were in a grocery store line behind a man wearing three earrings. Unable to control his curiosity, Zach asked him if it hurt to have the holes put in his ears.

The man smiled and replied, "A little but not a lot."

Zach said, "I would never do that, because I would say, 'Ow! Ow! Ow!' Anyhow, I wouldn't want to look like a girl."

Tree Huggers

The red maple tree in our front yard was in the process of dying, and some of the limbs were becoming brittle, so we decided to cut it down. When the twins overheard our plans, they threw a fit.

Eric argued, "Nan, you can't cut that tree down! It's our best climbing tree!"

Andrew chimed in, "Yeah, if you could just see the view from up there, you would never cut it down!"

I explained that we didn't like the idea of cutting the tree down either, but it was pretty much dead. Only a few leaves had come out on it this spring. A few mornings later, when I went out the front door, some new green growth on the maple caught my eye. Closer examination revealed that several small leaves had been stripped from a rhododendron bush along the side of the house and taped to the maple's branches.

You can't just crush that kind of dedication in a seven-year-old. We removed the brittle limbs and the maple got a one-year reprieve. By the next summer, the boys had found some more good climbing trees and had time to get used to the idea that the tree had to go.

Da...ad!

Zach asked if he could go over to Madison's house to play. Zach had been to her home a few times and his dad suggested it might be nice to call Madison's mother and ask if Madison could come over to his house to play.

Madison's mom said, "Not today. We're going shopping today, perhaps another time."

Still thinking about a way for Zach to play host, Rich suggested, "We could invite Madison to go skating or to a movie sometime. You know, it could be like a small date."

Zach was aghast. "Da...ad! That's so wrong! That's just sick! I'm only seven!"

Just because a seven-year-old's rules aren't written down doesn't mean he doesn't have them.

Discipline

Eric and Andrew had begun their second year of school. Beth and Andrew were doing the required parent-student review of the progressive discipline information sent home by the school. Level 1 was a reminder. At the top of the list was Level 4: a parent teacher conference, and level 5, referral to the Principal.

Andrew looked at his mother and said, "Well, you probably don't have to worry too much about levels 4 and 5."

Apparently, Andrew knew just how much he was willing to push the envelope with his behavior. A parent-teacher conference or the dreaded trip to the Principal's office was not on the list of things he was willing to risk by having a little fun at his teacher's expense. I don't remember what levels two and three were, but apparently they were well within his threshold for pain.

It's a Problem.

Eric and Andrew are usually inseparable, but sometimes they need a little space for themselves. Eight-year-old Andrew was having one of those days recently. I asked him, "Andrew, what is the hardest thing about being a twin?"

"Well, Nan, sometimes you would like to tell somebody that he's not really your brother, but you can't."

Don't Give Me the Bird Story.

Zach was quizzing Rich about how babies get here. "…And, Dad, I don't want the usual Birds and Bees, or Mommy and Daddy loved each other thing."

Rich began, "Babies start with an egg inside their mother…" He continued, tiptoeing through the fertilization and the development process in a manner designed to give a seven-year-old just enough information to head off more specific questions, which would be difficult to answer.

Sensing Rich's struggle, Zach said, "You don't have to tell me how they come out. I already know that."

A little surprised, Rich asked, "O. K. – How?"

"Oh, the mothers have a special place in the middle of their chest that opens up, and out pops the baby."

Instinctively, Rich started to correct him, but decided to save that for another day. *There's only so much information a child can absorb at one time. Maybe, I'll buy him a book, or maybe I'll tell him to ask his mother, or maybe….*

Levitra

As we pulled into Quinet's Restaurant parking lot for an after-church buffet, I heard eight-year-old Andrew from the rear seat.

"Levitra!" I wasn't sure what I heard, but a glance at Fred's face told me I was probably right.

Then, again from the rear seat, "Levitra. Levitra. Leviiiitra!"

I quietly asked Fred, "Should I ask him what he knows about Levitra?"

"Your call," was the grinning no-help response I got from him.

"Andrew, do you know what Levitra is?"

"Sure Nan. It's some kind of shampoo that you put on your hair, and it makes your hair stand up for three or four hours."

I had no further questions.

Roughing It

Son-in-law Mike had been on strike for about six months and through good money management he and Beth were able to keep their heads above water. They did however, caution their kids not to waste money on unnecessary things. It must have made a good impression! One day after school, Andrew asked me if he and Eric could have a milk shake. Not only did he ask but he also informed me of their plight - that they hadn't been allowed to waste money or put money into video machines or buy any unnecessary items. I observed that they hadn't had to give up their swimming pool, I-Pods and Game Boy Advances. But, being a good grandmother, I came to their rescue.

I PURCHASED THE MILK SHAKES! Andrew then said as he was sipping away, "You know Nan it's ok that we haven't had lots of treats because the Bible says in the afterlife, the poor will be rich and the rich will be poor, so we're going to be just fine."

Poor babies! I hope when they are older they never have to face being down to their last Mercedes.

That Night

Four years ago, Fred and I decided to remodel the house. Fred's version is, "The kids left home, so the house was too small, and we had to add on." That's only partially true. The kids left home several years ago, and they come home to visit with an ever-increasing number of grandchildren. Mr. Wisdom points out, this time correctly, "I have way more kids than when I had kids!"

Whatever the reason, we did it, and we decided to add a Jacuzzi room with thought of soaking our bones in our old age. The grandkids also enjoy bringing over their friends and relaxing among the bubbles. The Jacuzzi room has worked out well, and we have never regretted our decision with possible exception of *That Night*.

That Night began, as in many stories, as a dark and stormy night. Actually the storm was in the evening and ended with about an hour of daylight remaining. The twins headed off in the general direction of Grant's and Greg's houses to explore the aftermath of the storm. They returned about dark with three other boys in tow and asked to use the Jacuzzi. Without looking up from my book, I said, "Sure, why not?" My rhetorical question was to be answered within a matter of minutes. Alyssa walked by the Jacuzzi room and went directly to Fred's office and gave him a clue to the answer. "Grandfather, I think you had better come look at this."

My first clue was Fred walking briskly by my couch on his way to the Jacuzzi with a *not at all amused* look on his face. When he arrived, the explosion that ensued has become a legend on Fairview Drive. Ronnie, our next-door neighbor would later tell Fred, "Wow! I never even knew you had a temper!" Obviously, Ronnie is relatively new to the neighborhood. I have known about Fred's temper for over forty-seven years. Ronnie wasn't present when Fred's ladder jumped down a notch and went through the front window, showering the Christmas tree with glass ....or when I spent most of his paycheck on those darling pictures of our firstborn..... or when.... Never mind. I believe I've made my point.

At any rate, the explosion was followed by a rapid exodus of nine-year-old boys headed for home, the bathroom, the basement, wherever. Speed and distance from the Jacuzzi room seemed to be more important than destination. When I foolishly approached the Jacuzzi room, I saw Fred, eyes blazing at what appeared to be a three hundred gallon cup of hot chocolate and mumbling largely unintelligible phrases. The ones I could understand contained words like, "banned for life...at least until they're forty..." It seems the boys had been mud-sliding at Dead Man's Drop and hadn't showered before going into the Jacuzzi. There are times when it is not wise to try to make things better. This, I believe was one of those times.

"Do you want me to have the boys help?" I asked.

"No. If they come in here, I may grab one of them and use him to beat the other one, and I understand courts take a dim view of that sort of thing these days." This was followed by further mumbling having to do with courts obviously requiring judges to be childless.

Undeterred, I suggested, "It may not be as bad as it seems." The aftershock which followed the initial explosion convinced me that a retreat to my couch and the book I had been enjoying might be a great idea. Several hours and at least three refills later, the Jacuzzi water sparkled again. Fred was somewhat less than sparkling as he headed for bed, still mumbling phrases, now all too intelligible.

That was two years ago and things are somewhat better now. Fred has finally stopped the mandatory signed affidavits for boys entering the Jacuzzi, and I firmly believe he will get over the whole thing any decade now.

The Beauty of God's Creation

On long rides, and sometimes not so long rides, the boys get bored and restless. I have always tried to get them to look at the grandeur of God's creation when this happens – the clouds, the trees, the blue sky… This worked when they were younger, but now that they are old men of nine or ten, they have become jaded.

"Sure, Nan. Just look at the beautiful trees and flowers!" I know they are making fun of me, but I smile when I sometimes catch them looking.

Fred's method of dealing with their boredom is a bit more mundane. He has them count deer, most of which have met their demise along the road. The count carries some very specific rules: A live deer is equivalent to five dead ones. Anyone caught trying to sneak in a cow or a horse is penalized two deer. A deer in two piles still just counts as one. *That's disgusting!*

Strangely this game seems to hold their attention longer than trees, flowers and beautiful skies. There's no accounting for taste.

Zero $

Adults around the table were talking about the economy, the cost of living, and the difficulty that young couples just starting out must experience.

"Oh, I don't know," chimed in Andrew. "Sometimes I have zero dollars, and I get along just fine!"

True, he is fed and clothed by those who love him, but Andrew's young mind had grasped a valuable truth. Money isn't the primary source of happiness.

Library Bunny

The boys are growing up now. Since about ten, I have noticed an increased interest in members of the opposite sex. This is perfectly natural, and I'm happy to see it, but I think their machismo may need adjusted downward a notch or six.

We took Eric, Andrew, and Zach to Key Largo to swim and snorkel. After a morning at the beach, I heard the guys talking about that "English Muffin." I couldn't remember any snack of that nature. Slowly, I began to realize they were referring to the cute little British girl they had talked with on the beach. Later in the same day, they referred to a little dark-haired girl they had just met as a "Spanish Taco."

Unfortunately they haven't improved much over the past two years. More recently, when I picked Eric up after school, I saw Eric wave at a young girl. I asked what her name was.

"Don't know. She's a Library Bunny!"

When I ask Fred where the boys got their rather sexist attitudes, he just shrugs, with palms turned upward as a disclaimer. Personally, I think we still have a lot of work to do with about three generations of males in this family!

A Favorite Gift

February 4, 2007 – I'm sixty-two years old today. The entire world celebrated with me as it was Super Bowl Sunday. I love to attend local high school football games, but watching a game on TV isn't the same. I think the commercials tend to distract me. The Super Bowl commercials, however, are great. I do find myself wondering how much good all that money would do if it was spent to help the needy. Fred says I just don't understand capitalism, that sales create jobs that do benefit the needy. There are just some holes in the system that we need to patch. He's right about the holes for sure.

We had a wonderful Super Bowl dinner at daughter Beth's house – pizza, chips and dip, ice cream cake, all good stuff. Mike, Beth, Eric, Andrew, Fred and my mother all did a creditable job on the munchies. It was great to have Mom there. She's going through her terrible eighty-twos and I'm going through my terrible sixty-twos. That's a lot of years!

We decided to watch the second half at home in order to be closer to our bed when the game was over. When we arrived, the calls to wish me a happy birthday started. I talked a while to Rich, and then Zach got on the phone and said, "Happy Birthday, Nan! Please hang up so I can give you a birthday message on your answering machine." Birthdays are a time for looking forward and also looking back. I pondered how our ancestors might react to the concept of an answering machine.

"So, you have to have a machine now to talk to someone?" Anyhow, I agreed and after Zach cautioned me several times not to pick up the phone, I let it ring four times and heard the answering machine:

"Happy birthday to you. Cha-Cha-Cha! Happy birthday to you. Cha-Cha-Cha! Happy birthday, dear Nanny. Happy birthday to you. Cha-Cha-Cha! Have a happy sixty..? Have a happy birthday. You're quite old now. Sixty…two. Happy birthday. I love you! Bye."

I sent him a grandmother's blessing as I silently prayed that he might live long enough to have a grandson call him and tell him he's getting really old and wish him a happy birthday. It actually felt pretty good.

Sleepover

Nothing strikes fear into the heart of a grandmother like hearing the dreaded "sleepover" word. The twins often spend the night with us, and often as not, ask to have someone sleep over. Since they are twins, this usually involves two *someones* and twice the trouble. Typically, I say yes approximately six hours before screaming, "Never again!"

The problem is bedtime. It's not so much getting into bed as it is turning off the light, staying in bed, and actually going to sleep. The concept of going to sleep seems to be a bit beyond the grasp of an eleven-year-old. During a recent sleepover, I instructed the boys to turn off the lights by midnight, and went to bed myself. I awakened at two thirty and decided to check on them. They were in their bedroom alright, surrounded by chips and candy, eyes glued to the TV. Every light in the house was on. A bucket of melted ice cream was in the kitchen, along with candy wrappers and remnants of cheese and summer sausage. I don't know why they don't just call them *eatovers.*

This time I stuck to my "Never again" for a couple of weeks, so the guys pulled an end run and moved the sleepover to Bonnie's house. Bonnie is the neighborhood east-side resident grandmother and 911 communicator. I warned Bonnie that the boys would try to con her and stay up all night. The guys were smooth with Bonnie. Her grandson asked if she had a lullaby they could put in their Boom Box to listen to until they fell asleep. Only an eleven-year-old would use lullaby and Boom Box in the same sentence. Andrew said he was hoping for something from Mozart or Chopin. Bonnie said she had never had that request before. Finally she came up with a CD with the sound of falling rain. Amazingly, it worked. The guys actually went to sleep.

I'm so jealous and have been looking for a good rainfall CD ever since.

The Post-Mortem

If you believe, *Beauty must suffer,* try science.

"Nan," Andrew asked from somewhere in another room, "Can you identify an animal by looking at its skeleton?"

I asked but really didn't want to know, "Where is the skeleton?"

"Here in your bathroom sink. Come look, Nan."

My worst fears were confirmed when I arrived at the bathroom. There, looking up at me were two bony eye sockets, various vertebrae, legs and toes, complete with claws. Either a rat or a squirrel had met its demise and ended up in my bathroom sink. For some reason, I preferred to think, *squirrel.* I'm not sure what I said, but after regaining my composure, I remember saying, "Get that skeleton out of my sink!"

As I reached for the Clorox, I heard Andrew open the front door and announce proudly to his buddies waiting outside, "Squirrel!"

I tried not to think about his next project.

Trick or Treat

I think the twins, at eleven years old, are approaching the age limit for trick or treat, although we used to have a couple of retirees who would take martini glasses and go door to door.

Last Halloween, Andrew grabbed a Wal-Mart bag and headed for the door. "Whoa!" yelled Beth, "Aren't you supposed to dress up as someone to go trick or treating? Where's your costume?"

"I have it on, Mom. I'm going as Eric."

Cows and Udder Things

We were in Allentown visiting Zach and Rich. It was the morning before Zach's soccer game and Rich was fixing breakfast. Zach was drinking his milk, put down the glass and said, "Nan, isn't it funny how a cow eats green grass and out comes white milk?"

Always glad to help a grandson with a science or life lesson, I sketched a grazing cow with four stomachs and an udder on my napkin. "Zach," I said, "It must be a difficult problem, because God provided the cow with four stomachs and an udder to turn green grass into milk." The anatomy lesson must have triggered another memory.

Zach, who lives next door to two doctors and their children, said, "Nan, yesterday, over at Alec's house we did an in depth study of the vagina." Rich looked straight ahead and kept turning pancakes. Fred and I avoided looking at each other, but when I did sneak a peek, Fred had a smile that looked suspiciously as if another childhood memory had just been triggered.

I simply said, "That's nice." No more questions were asked and we just ate breakfast much as I've always suspected normal people might.

The Rest of the Story

Since Eric and Andrew live nearby and sleep over frequently, for the last five years or so they have had their own room in our house. They have twin beds with steel tubing frames.

"There, let them try to tear those up," I remember Fred saying when we bought them.

Unfortunately the legs have plastic caps on each end to close the open ends of the tubing. Time after time we would find one of the caps off when we went into their room. We told them there was no reason to take the beds apart, and we couldn't understand why they would repeatedly remove the caps. After many requests to leave the caps in place yielded no results, Fred put a rubber snake in one of the legs and replaced the cap. The next time the boys visited, we settled in and waited to hear a scream from the bedroom. After a few minutes, Eric sauntered casually into the room twirling the serpent in one hand and asked, "Hey. Who put the rubber snake in our candy safe?"

The Sex Goddess

Jackson read the birthday card his father had given his mother:

To my wife
Thank you for all the great meals.
Thank you for being a great mother.
And Especially
(inside)
For being a sex goddess!

Jackson asked, "Grandmother, what is a sex goddess?" I stalled a bit to give myself time to come up with an answer appropriate for a seven-year-old.

"Well, Jackson, it means your dad finds your mom attractive. She's a woman and he likes the way she looks." That seemed to satisfy Jackson, and there was no further discussion about it until I repeated the story to Fred on the way home. I had forgotten the twins were with us on the trip until Andrew piped up from the back seat.

"Grandmother, when I get married, I want a smokin' hot Mama that can cook!"

Fred replied, "That works for me, but I know some guys that have been burned pretty badly by that kind of thinking."

Men! I think it's a phase they go through from about seven to eighty or so – or death. I should have worked more on an answer appropriate for an eleven and a sixty-five year-old.

Creative Movements

Our recent South Carolina trip to visit grandkids happily coincided with "Grandparents' Day" at Jacob's pre-school. Being well qualified, we accepted the invitation to attend. We were greeted by a priest and ushered into a small cheerful room where the children presented a brief program, and where each of us was able to observe that our grandchild was just a bit brighter than the rest. This was apparently acceptable so long as we did so quietly.

Then Jacob led us to a room for refreshments, one of his specialties.

Sometime after refreshments were served, I asked where the restrooms were located. Following a teacher's directions, I came to the bathroom door, which had a sign declaring in large letters, "CREATIVE MOVEMENTS". I chuckled to myself. Rejoining the group, I commented to the teachers on the cute sign.

"Oh," they said in unison, "That's the name of our school!"

OH GOD!

It's not Easy

Our pastor delivered a sermon about worshiping idols. Our son Rich, who was about four at the time, said he didn't understand what the pastor was talking about. I tried to explain to him that sometimes people would make a golden calf or some strange image and bow down and worship it. I explained that we should worship God, even though it wasn't always easy. I asked if he understood.

He said, "Oh yeah, Mom, I get it! It's hard to wash up God. He's way too big to put in a bathtub."

Michelangelo I'm Not

Craig showed some talent for art at an early age. When he was twelve, his teacher encouraged him to enter an art contest sponsored by the PTA. He had seen pictures of wild turkeys in an outdoor magazine, and decided he would like to do a painting of a wild turkey. We soon discovered he was also a very temperamental artist. Day after day he would become dissatisfied with his work and threaten to tear it up. We thought it was pretty good and pressured him to complete what he had started. He finally finished the painting before the deadline. He won the county and state competitions and earned honorable mention in the national contest.

Some weeks later our pastor told us she had seen Craig's work and asked him if he would do a sketch of the outside of the church that she could use on the cover of the weekly bulletin. She knew he loved to draw, and she was surprised when he was reluctant and seemed to be avoiding her after she made the request.

We learned that an artist's perception may be a little different. When we asked Craig why he wouldn't go along with what appeared to be a fairly modest request, he said, "Mom, do you have any idea how many bricks are in that church?" I laughed as I realized that, unlike the simple one-line sketch the pastor had in mind, Craig's concept of the project was a very detailed drawing which would take him six months of hard work.

King of the Juice

Aly's parents took her to church most Sundays. They always sat in a small side-chapel near the rear of the sanctuary so they could make a quick exit if needed. Fred and I would usually sit near them in case Grandma's assistance was required.

On one Lenten Sunday, Aly was coloring one of those pictures that were provided to keep a three-year-old busy and quiet during the sermon. The pastor made reference to the "King of the Jews", and Aly perked up immediately.

"JUICE," she exclaimed! "I LOVE JUICE! APPLE JUICE! ORANGE JUICE! I LOVE ALL KINDS OF JUICE!"

The pastor tried briefly to regain control, but wisely decided just to go with the moment. When the laughter finally subsided, he commented that it was good that at least someone was listening to the sermon.

I Know Jesus

Eric and Andrew were taken to church regularly, and they formed strong theological opinions by the time they were three years old. The following scene would be repeated every Sunday for months: Pastor Brian had an olive complexion and sported a dark beard. When he entered the sanctuary at the beginning of the service, one of the twins would point and say, "There's Jesus,"

I would explain to them, "No Honey, That's Pastor Carpenter. He looks a little like Jesus and he works for him, but that's Pastor Carpenter." The boys would nod as though they understood. When Brian reached the front of the church, he would sit down behind the pulpit where he was no longer visible to the twins, and they would become occupied with other things.

The pastor would reappear when he stood for the opening hymn. The first twin to spot him would look at the other and declare knowingly, "Jesus is back."

When we told Pastor Brian the twins were convinced he was Jesus, he said, "Trying to live up to that assignment will put a lot of pressure on me, but I will take it seriously and try always to set a good example for them."

Field Trips

I asked Andrew if he was planning to attend Bible School the following week.

"What's Bible School, Nan?"

"It's a lot like Sunday School, Andrew, except you have more time for crafts and singing and learning about Jesus."

"Nope! Not going, Nan. I already went to church once this week."

The following week, Andrew relented and attended every day, and told his grandfather he had a good time. His teacher, Linda, told us he did decline one activity though. She had announced to the class, "Today we are going to visit three towns that Jesus visited – Nazareth, Capernaum and Jerusalem." Immediately, Andrew's hand shot up. "What is it Andrew?"

"I can't go Mrs. Frizell. Mom says I have to stay inside the church, no matter what, until she comes to pick me up."

Let the Little Children…

When Zach was five, Dad was away on a business trip and his mom, Melanie, had to work, so I answered the call and flew to Allentown to take care of Zach. Melanie had Sunday off, so she and Zach and I attended church. It was a beautiful communion service. Later that evening, Beth called.

When Zach answered the phone, she asked him how his day had been.

"Great! We went to church and I drank Jesus!"

That reminded me of another communion story when four-year-old Laura Rose exclaimed to a nearby parishioner, "My, wasn't the blood really good today?" Both stories bring quickly to mind "Let the little children come to me." Also they are reminders that God always meets us where we are at the time, not necessarily where a group of theologians might think we should be.

Pressure

Eric and Andrew always say their prayers with Mom at bedtime. It was near Christmas and after their prayer session, Andrew asked Beth, "Is God always watching us?"

"Yes." Beth replied.

"And Jesus?"

"Yes." She tucked the boys in and went to bed herself. A few minutes later Andrew was standing by her bedside.

"Mom, does Santa Claus see everything we do?"

"I suppose so. Now please go to bed."

Andrew trotted off to bed but was back five minutes later. "Mom?"

"Yes, Andrew."

"Do you remember last summer at the beach when you were taking a shower, and baby Jackson woke up and started crying?"

Beth didn't remember but she said, "Yes," just to avoid extending the conversation further. "What about it Andrew?"

"Well, I woke him up to see what he would do."

With all that surveillance, a five-year-old can't be too careful at Christmas time.

Repentance

Most Sundays, a brief children's sermon, with the children gathered around the pastor, is a highlight of our worship service. Last Sunday, the pastor explained that sin involved doing things we are not supposed to do. He then asked the children how many times they had sinned during the past week. With a worried expression, Eric raised his hand and blurted out, "So many times I've lost track!"

Somewhat nervous laughter spread through the congregation. It was likely that several members were remembering times when they too had lost track.

Is Heaven in the Ground?

Aunt Louise was an elementary schoolteacher who touched many young lives during her forty-seven-year career. Even in retirement, she tutored neighborhood children. There was never a charge, and she always served a snack. Andrew and I visited her grave in the spring, about two years after her death. Andrew, usually a chatterbox, was unusually quiet and thoughtful. I think he sensed somehow that this was a serious occasion. As I placed flowers near her headstone, he asked quietly, "Is she there, Nanny?"

I told him, "No. Her body is here, but she's in heaven now."

"Is heaven in the ground, Nanny?"

I was moved by Andrew's question, and I tried to focus my mind on what I really believed about life and death, and how to explain it in terms that a five-year-old would understand. Aunt Louise had died at ninety-seven, and she had suffered ill health for years, so being able to pass from this world had freed her from all that. I told Andrew that we weren't sure where heaven is, but her soul, the part that made her Aunt Louise, was somewhere peaceful, with no pain or suffering. He seemed satisfied with that answer.

When I told Fred this story, he thought Aunt Louise would have loved Andrew's question and was inspired to write the following poem:

IS HEAVEN in the GROUND, NANNY?

Grandma took young Andrew to visit Aunt Louise's grave.
"Is she there Nanny?"
"No Honey, she's in heaven"
"Aunt Louise was a wonderful lady, Drew.
She spent forty-seven years in one-room schools teaching short people like you.
Her smile was quick – She served cookies and milk to students in tutoring sessions.
She made learning a game and fun for the young.
She knew the importance of early impressions.
She had a love of living and a penchant for giving, and I know you don't remember.
But her body wore out, and we brought her here two years ago September.
We placed her here beneath the grass, but now she rests in heaven."
"Is heaven in the ground, Nanny?"
Silence filled the air, save for the sound of theologians running for cover.
"Good question, Drew, but now you leave me the task
Of giving you an answer as honest as the question you asked.
Truth is, Drew, we don't know where heaven is – we're not even sure it's a place.
It just as well may be, the way we must travel to save the human race.

A timeless question asked, for we can never know with certainty
About things after our death or matters approaching eternity.
Aunt Louise would have loved your question – I can almost hear her laughter.
That's the kind of honest inquiry that she was always after.
I don't know where heaven is, but this I know is true.
As long as there are boys with minds like yours, her spirit lives on in you.
Great question, Andrew, for one two years shy of seven.
Come here young man and take my hand.
You're joy enough 'til I find heaven."

Whatever You Ask…

Usually, when the twins spend the night with us, the day ends with bedtime prayers. Many times, after a day with them, I need prayer more than they do. A six-year-old boy's prayers are often lengthy and artful. Just to be thorough, many times Eric ends his prayer with a blanket petition, "And God, please answer every prayer that has ever been prayed."

Andrew's prayers range from the mundane to thoughtful stewardship.

"Thank you God for all of my parts and the things that come out of them."

"Help us to use our natural resources and keep them clean."

Many times, I have to suppress that smile or laughter. I never want to close that little window into their most sincere thoughts.

By the Book

Andrew, at seven years, loved to play the piano. He didn't have the discipline to sit through lessons, but he played by ear and would seldom pass by a piano without playing something. One afternoon after school, I was in the kitchen and Andrew was happily playing in the next room. I heard a loud bang and rushed in to check on him.

"Andrew, are you all right?"

"Sure, Nan," he said, holding up a hymnbook. "The Holy Hymenal just fell down."

"Andrew," I said, trying to maintain control. "I think that's Holy Hymnal, Buddy."

Jesus Saves

Each summer, three generations of Goddards, mates, and occasionally friends and extended family descend on Ocean City Maryland for a week or two of sea, sand and fun. It is said that when your children reach a certain age, they no longer want to go on vacations with you. Our children are presently forty-five, forty-three and forty-one. They say they will let us know when that happens. Days are usually for fishing, crabbing, swimming, or sunning on the beach. Evenings are, often as not, for the boardwalk. The kids play volleyball or beach football, and the adults people-watch and graze on funnel cakes, fries, ice cream or other healthy choices.

There is a very talented sand sculptor who sets up shop near the southern end of the boardwalk. His sculptures always carry a religious theme. Each day he creates a new Biblical scene and has it ready for the evening boardwalk crowd. He places a bucket for donations and a pile of give-away cards or trinkets nearby. Some years ago, eight-year-olds Eric, Andrew and Zach spent several minutes quietly gazing at the sculptor's depiction of Jesus. I think it was the first time they really saw his work, although they had passed by it many times over the years.

They each picked up a little silver colored plastic cross from the give-away pile. The vertical part of the cross was inscribed, "Jesus saves." The cross bar read, "John 3:16."

Zach asked what the inscription meant. Without hesitation, Andrew replied, "It means Jesus saves John at 3:16."

They weren't sure if the event was 3:16 a.m. or p.m. At any rate, they probably had missed witnessing the saving, so they went to play volleyball instead.

Hallelujah!

We traveled to Allentown to visit son Rich and grandson Zach, now ten. On Sunday morning, we decided to attend church with them. On the five-mile trip to church, Zach kept muttering a constant protest from the back seat. "I hate church! Why do we have to go to church? I'm not going. The pastor's sermons are way too long! Boring! Stupid church!"

About half way there, I couldn't resist a comment and mini-sermon of my own. I told Zach church was good for him and he would become a better boy by going. Zach continued his protest, ignoring my comments. I thought that at any moment, Rich was going to reprimand or quiet him down, but Zach continued grumbling and Rich just kept driving.

We parked and Zach led the way into the church. Rich turned to me and said, "Just watch, Mom." To my surprise, Zach picked the third row from the front and sat right in the center looking at the church stage. Not exactly the choice you would expect from a child who has just been dragged mumbling and grumbling to church. The service was a blend of praise and traditional worship. When the band and praise team started a spirited number, I noticed a rapid change in Zach. He was singing, swaying, dancing and clapping his hands, really getting into the service. A smile and a look of complete happiness were on his face. I wondered *Is this how the Holy Spirit works?* It certainly appeared to have descended on Zach.

When I mentioned this to Rich, he just smiled and said, "Happens every week, Mom."

Caleb

…and a little child shall lead them – *Isaiah 11:6*

That passage from Isaiah foretells the mission of Jesus, who also had a lot to say about children of all ages. It also applies to Caleb, a member of the gang, who lives just across the street. Caleb is happy, thoughtful and soft-spoken, at least as soft-spoken as is possible for an eleven-year-old. He can smell a party or an adventure a mile away and always shows up with a hat, costume or appropriate equipment for the task at hand. Caleb is up for just about anything. Caleb also provides strong moral leadership for the gang.

If the guys outside are feuding or the language turns bad, Caleb comes in and says, "Mrs. G, the guys are fighting," or "They're saying bad words out there." This is my cue to open the back door and restore order or tell them to clean up the language.

Caleb quickly rejoins the group, and his disclosure is never held against him. The gang seems to respect his position as self-appointed chaplain. It's as though they sense that they really need the service he provides. It strikes me that some of us big kids could take a lesson from Caleb's example of standing up for what is right. Needless to say, Caleb is always welcome at our house.

Confirmation

Eric and Andrew attended confirmation class at our church this year. Andrew was concerned and asked his mother if he wasn't sure that he was ready to become a full member of the church at conclusion of the class, would he have to stand before the congregation and say so. Beth told him not to worry. He would not have to do that. I told her that I would have told him, "Yes." A little fear can be an effective motivator. The twins are a couple of bright, but sometimes irreverent teenagers. I cautioned them to listen and be on their best behavior in class. I think they tried, but they couldn't resist the fun of challenging the pastor about many of the church's beliefs and traditions.

"What makes holy water holy? Isn't all water holy?"

"Root beer is mostly water. If I am baptized in root beer, does it count?"

"Why are there Ten Commandments? Are you sure we have found them all?"

The pastor said he enjoyed their enthusiasm and questions. That may be true, but personally, I'm sure there were moments when he wanted to strangle them. At any rate, they completed their classes. They both affirmed their baptisms and officially became members of the church on Palm Sunday.

As the pastor prepared communion on a Sunday shortly after their confirmations, he told the congregation if anyone wanted to pause at the altar rail to pray after receiving the elements, they were welcome to do so. As I knelt at the altar rail for a quiet moment of prayer, I became aware of Eric and Andrew on either side of me.

Eric whispered, "What should I pray for?"

I said, "Give thanks for everything."

Andrew asked quietly, "Is it okay, Nanny?" I nodded my head. Oh yes! It was more than okay. What greater joy than to be at prayer with two of my grandsons.

God Bless America

Eva had learned to sing "God Bless America" in pre-school. When her family joined us in Ocean City for vacation, she announced that she just HAD to sing "God Bless America" every time she saw an American flag. We thought her compulsion to sing was adorable, but we had forgotten that it was the Fourth of July.

We remembered that many businesses and homes displayed the flag on the Fourth, but we had never really noticed just how many. We soon realized that Eva was true to her word and sang EVERY time she saw the flag. She sang her way from one end of the boardwalk to the other. She sang in the car from Assateague Island to the Delaware line. She sang for family, police officers, and complete strangers, anyone who would listen. She sang loudly and seldom missed a note or a word. We thought the first hundred renditions were precious - the second hundred, not so much.

But when I saw the faces of those people who listened intently to a little four-year-old patriot belting out "God Bless America" it was like I too was hearing it for the first time, and I quickly regained my proud grandmother status. God bless America – Indeed!

The Blessing

During a visit, Craig and Gina were enjoying a dinner out. Fred and I kept Jackson, Jacob and Eva. We ordered carry-out from a local Mexican restaurant. Fred and Jackson arrived with the food while I was upstairs bathing Eva, and Jacob was in his room playing *Rock Band.*

Jackson and Fred were hungry and grew tired of waiting for us, so they decided to start eating. When Eva, Jacob and I finally arrived to begin eating, Eva looked at Jackson and Fred and announced very loudly, "You forgot the blessing!"

"No we didn't," Jackson countered, "We said grace before you came in."

"Well, I wasn't here, so put the covers back on the plates. We have to pray together." After one unsuccessful attempt to pray without re-covering the carry-out containers, we put the lids back on and prayed together.

Jackson prayed that we would survive Eva.

I Think It's in Leviticus

Steve and Margaret are fellow grandparents in good standing. Margaret related the following story about four-year-old grandson Caleb:

During a visit, Caleb spotted a wonderful Transformer, not well enough hidden, in a closet. Caleb asked, "Grammy, whose Transformer is this?"

I couldn't think of a good cover story fast enough. I decided the cat was out of the bag, and I had just as well fess up. I said, "Caleb, that will be your Transformer on your birthday. Sometimes when we know you really like something, Grandpa and I buy it ahead of time. Then if the store runs out of them, we will already have one for you."

"Can I have it now?"

"No, Honey. You have to wait for your birthday."

To a four-year-old, even a few hours seems forever. So, every morning Caleb made another attempt. "Can I have my Transformer now?" We hated to keep saying no, and we bought some little Transformers, hoping that would satisfy him until his birthday. Nothing worked. On about day three or four, Caleb gave it one last shot.

"Grammy, you know, it even says in the Bible, that if you find your birthday present early, you should get it on the same day you find it."

Widows Might, but not Me

The little children in my Sunday school class brought some coins each week for our collection. One Sunday a little girl put a penny in the plate. Another child said, "Hey, she only put in a penny!"

"That's all I have!" said the little girl.

I thought, what a wonderful opportunity for the parable of the widow's mite! I happily retold that wonderful old story of the widow who gave the smallest of coins, but Jesus said she had given the most of all because she gave all that she had. The children grew silent as they reflected on the meaning of the story.

Just as they were leaving the class, someone spotted a penny on the floor.

"That's mine!" exclaimed the little girl who had given the penny. She quickly scooped up the penny and dropped it in her change purse before anyone else could claim it. As she opened her purse, I saw at least a dozen coins in it.

"I'm going to buy some candy!" she shouted as she ran down the hall.

Oh well. Maybe next year….

Thus Sayeth the Lord…

At the church youth group meeting, the teens were in the middle of a spirited discussion about the proper roles of men and women in the church and in the world. One young lady was passionately pressing her case for equal treatment of women. "Why is it that guys get all the opportunity for big careers and get to do all the exciting things in the world? Women are expected to stay home, cook, clean and raise kids. Why is that? It's not fair!"

Unable to resist the opening, young Jim declared, "It says right here in Leviticus, 'Ye big breasted shall do the housework.' "

Mickey, a late bloomer and secretary of the group, without looking up from her notes, declared wistfully, "Well, I guess that leaves me out."

I'M FINE.
HAS ANYONE SEEN MY
LEG ANYWHERE?

Reckless Behavior

We became conditioned to children's reckless behavior and runs to the emergency room early in our married life. I have always believed this behavior came from Fred's side of the family. He denies it, of course, but his times of screaming down a mountain road on his bicycle do not help his case much. By the time Rich and Craig were six and four they were on a first name basis with all the emergency room doctors at St. Mary's Hospital. The doctors were beginning to look at us strangely, and I'm sure that if it were today we would be the subject of a thorough child abuse investigation.

One instance that comes to mind is Craig's trip to the ER after he kicked at a pebble and fell, striking his head on the pavement and opening up a small but nasty gash. The ER doctor asked him, "Didn't I sew you up last week?"

"No, that was my brother."

When the doctor said, "Well, this is going to require a couple of stitches to close it up," Craig became hysterical.

"No! I don't want sewn up! No stitches!"

When the doctor asked Craig if he gave him a Tootsie Pop, would Craig allow him to put in the stitches, Craig said happily, "okay."

I couldn't believe it! After all that kicking and screaming, the little fink sold out for a Tootsie Pop. Perhaps that was the point where we became a little more relaxed about emergency room runs. Don't get me wrong. We're not blasé about it, but when the injury is not life threatening or likely to result in permanent injury, we try not to overreact. That's a good thing. We didn't get burned out on Beth's bicycle wreck, Zach's fall against the tub in the bathroom or his diving board incident, or Andrew's severely spraining his wrist falling in the woods. (We suspect an un-confessed four-wheeler wreck.) We were able to save our concern for the bigger ticket items, like Eric's concussion, following a slam dunk attempt on an icy basketball court.

Battle Scars

My belief that the twins were hunters or warriors in a former life is strengthened by their love of fighting with plastic swords and knives. They take great pride in their bruises and battle scars. At age four, they make up and tell elaborate war stories about how they got them. At the end of one hard day of combat, Andrew came into the house with bruises and scratch marks all over his face.

"Andrew, what happened?" I asked.

Without hesitation – "These three guys from Moundsville came down with knives and weapons and did this to me."

"Andrew," I said, "Who really scratched your face? I don't think it was three guys from Moundsville."

"Eric," was the reply.

I couldn't imagine.

Football

We took the twins, then four-years-old, to the local high school football game. We sat on the visitors' side since it is more suitable for small children. The bleachers extend all the way to ground-level, and there is a grassy area between the bleachers and the field where little guys who get bored with watching the game can play.

It took Eric and Andrew the better part of thirty seconds into the first half to become bored and join their friends in the grassy area for their own games of football, Stomp the Empty Soda Bottle, and Just Tackle Whomever is Handy. After the game, I asked a badly scratched-up Andrew how he liked the game.

"It was o.k. Nan, but there was just too much fighting!"

We had observed their play closely enough to see that Andrew had not exclusively played the role of *Fightee*. He had managed to get in his share of the licks too. The next week, grounds keepers had spread some sand as a first step to repairing the area where the grass was pretty much trampled out. Gleefully, the little guys added the game of Throw the Sand to their repertoire and, had at it, shortly after the kickoff. Once again, we observed, there was entirely too much fighting.

Fight

Zach arrived for the Christmas holiday to a welcome of high fives all the way around. He and Eric and Andrew radiated a mischievous happiness as only five-year-old boys can. The euphoria continued until the next afternoon when we heard a blood-curdling scream coming from the playroom. Procedure dictates that everyone run in the direction of the scream. When the scream emanates from a two-boy group, we usually find one boy wounded and one hiding. If a three-boy group is involved, expect one wounded, one offering consolation and one hiding. In this case, Zach was wounded, Andrew was consoling and Eric was hiding. This was almost too easy to solve. The wound wasn't serious and the nature of the argument was never disclosed.

The next morning Zach looked at his swollen lip in the mirror and declared, "I never want to see Eric again!" Obviously the bruise went a bit deeper than his lip. Eric had apologized, but his sincerity was suspect.

Under his breath so Grandma couldn't hear, "Well Zach, now you know who is the toughest." Grandma did hear, and the remark bought Eric some additional time out, tacked on to his original sentence for hitting Zach. I kept the boys separated for most of the day.

About 2 p.m. Zach said, "I'm ready to play with Eric and Andrew again." The lip looked better. Penance had been done and harmony had been restored within the tribe. The fight was over, but I know it won't be the last.

Loophole

One autumn afternoon, I was watching the kids after school. Eric and Andrew were outside playing. First-graders can get into trouble in no time, so I checked on them frequently. Not surprisingly, my third check found them about eighteen feet up in a large pine tree, and heading higher. I made them come down and lectured them concerning the variety of body parts they could bruise, fracture or otherwise damage if they fell.

"Aw, Nanny," they argued, "We're climbers!" I told them that I could plainly see that, but I marked off with my hand a height in the pine that they were allowed to go, and no higher. Under threat of being confined to the house, they agreed to my terms and came down to that level. I returned to the house to prepare dinner. Within five minutes, Eric burst through the door, gasping for breath.

"Come quick, Nan! Andrew has his foot caught in a tree!" As I ran I pictured Andrew hanging upside-down with only one foot holding him. To my relief, when I got there, next-door neighbor, Gary, had Andrew securely in his grasp. He had climbed up and rescued Andrew, this time from a nearby oak tree.

Andrew was still crying as I took his hand and was leading him back to the house. Because of the seriousness of the offense, I gave him a bit of a lecture. "Andrew, I can't believe you did that, just after you promised to go no higher than we agreed!"

"But, Nan," Andrew sobbed, "The problem is, you never gave us instructions for that particular tree!"

Double Indemnity?

Eight-year-old Zach was preparing to go on his first snowboarding trip with his father. He phoned his mother and asked, "Mom, do I have life insurance?"

When she said that he did, he said, "Maybe you should consider upping it."

Turtle Attack

One fall morning after Fred had left for work, I poured myself a cup of coffee and sat down to relax a few minutes before tackling my to do list. The front door burst open and a breathless Andrew shot through. "Nanny, come quick! Come quick, Nanny!"

"What's wrong, Andrew?"

"A turtle has Eric and won't let him go!"

I jumped into the car with Andrew and sped toward the alleged turtle ambush. No problem locating Eric. I heard him before I saw him, and when I ran over to him, sure enough, a turtle had Eric and wouldn't let him go. The boys had been on their way to school when Eric tried to pick up a box turtle. He reached a little too far forward and got one finger under the hinged portion of the turtle's shell. When the turtle retreated inside his shell, it clamped down on Eric's finger. Eric was screaming bloody murder, and the turtle wasn't about to come out to see what the ruckus was all about. Fred keeps a few tools in the trunk of the car, so I was able to grab a screwdriver and apply enough pressure to pry Eric's finger loose. The skin wasn't broken, so I took the Eric home and cleaned the bruised area and took the boys to school.

"Neat!" declared Andrew, "Now we have a turtle for show and tell!"

No Doctors Please

Andrew, nearly eleven now, will try anything that requires a ball, wheels, a helmet or an ankle wrap. I have watched him take hits on the football field or on his skateboard (more accurately "off" his skateboard) that take a grandmother's breath away. He sheds no tears and offers no complaint of pain. Doctors however, are a different story. Any mention of a shot, throat culture or fluoride application sets off a panic and intense resistance. "NO WAY! NOT DOIN' IT! NOT NOW! NOT EVER!"

Andrew's position on the medical profession was formed by the time he was three years old. Following a series of sore throats, influenza, and assorted viruses, Andrew exclaimed as his mother turned once more into the hospital parking lot, "I'm not going in there. That place is dangerous!"

The Fort

School's out and the neighborhood gang members have been busy with their first summer project, the fort. The fort looks a bit like Gilligan's Island comes to Appalachia, consisting of small logs stacked in lean-to fashion, topped by smaller branches and some makeshift thatch. Construction progressed nicely in a wooded area that grows poison ivy abundantly. After a couple of weeks, the fort was topped out with thatch about the same time Eric, Andrew, Caleb and Grant were topped out with Calamine lotion.

The fort was commissioned, and all was well until a parent's inspection uncovered a makeshift fire pit where the natives had roasted some crayfish. A couple of kids got voted off the island by the parents' council. Others were discouraged by stories about snakes coming out to sun themselves on the rocks this time of year. It was also mentioned that the rabid raccoon population was up significantly. I think the parents who told those stories knew they were effective because they heard them from their parents twenty years ago.

Whether from caution or the short attention span of eleven-year-olds, we haven't seen any smoke from the hillside lately, and the gang is now occupied with skateboarding and baseball. No harm. No foul.

Dead Man's Drop

We live on Fairview Drive, in a quiet neighborhood that has cycled from wall-to-wall kids, to no kids and back again to wall-to-wall kids since we have been here. Near the end of Fairview Drive lives Bonnie, a kindly grandmother who is a retired teacher, volunteer reader at the school and also aids and abets the gang. Her two grandsons, Chase and Grant are gang members, along with our grandsons Eric and Andrew. Caleb and Greg are also regulars, as are all of the middle school guys who live on or near Fairview. That's the permanent membership, but a few visitors rotate in and out, depending on whether or not they are grounded at the time.

The gang is into anything that requires wheels, a helmet, grind-rail, an ankle wrap or food. In short, they love outside sports and inside messing up. That's where the aiding and abetting come in, usually consisting of food, first aid and cleanup. Bonnie has the east end of the block. I have the west. In addition, Bonnie is winter 911 Communicator. That's because Dead Man's Drop is in her end of the neighborhood. Dead Man's Drop is the gang's makeshift snowboard park constructed on a steep lot that is vacant except for a few trees spaced just widely enough apart to allow for the buildup of lethal speed between crashes.

I have summer 911duty because the skateboard park is in my driveway. We use a lot of Band Aids and ice for sprained ankles or bloody noses. Fortunately first aid has been sufficient to date, and we haven't had to make any phone calls.

There have been no broken bones, a fact that continues to amaze Fred. He recently got to observe Dead Man's Drop in action when he went to tell Eric and Andrew their mother had called and said it was time for them to come home. He arrived in time to see Andrew shoot down the slope, which had gotten icy from overuse. He skidded and hit the ramp sideways, did a vertical 225, and landed on his head and shoulders. After what was probably two seconds but seemed an eternity, a hand and two little fingers shot skyward in a signal that is universally understood by the gang, and that I believe is loosely translated, "I'm fine! Has anyone seen my leg anywhere?"

More than a little alarmed, Fred gathered the gang for a cautionary word.

"Hey guys, when the pro snowboarders practice their maneuvers, have you noticed they do it with three feet or so of powder base to cushion their fall, not on four inches of snow on hard frozen ground? You might want to think about that."

"Sure Mr. G. You're probably right," someone conceded as the next candidate for the emergency room shot down the icy slope toward the ramp. After he had picked himself up and regained his breath, the gang decided they had enough for the day and headed off to Bonnie's for some hot chocolate and french fries.

Whatever Works

Eric and Andrew's father gave them four-wheelers to ride when they were thirteen. They keep them in our garage because our house is closer to the trails than their father Dave's house. Unwittingly, we became the adult supervisors for the riding. We were concerned because we thought thirteen was a little young to turn these guys loose on four-wheelers. We always cautioned them to ride slowly and responsibly. They always respond with, "We know. We're fine."

One evening Fred heard engines revving in the back yard. Upon investigation, he found the two boys doing wheelies, and obviously competing to see who could go the farther distance on two wheels. Andrew's turn ended with the four-wheeler completely vertical and Andrew standing behind it, holding on to the handlebars. Fred shut down the game immediately and growled at the boys, "What do you think you are doing? That's a good way to get yourself killed by a four-wheeler landing on top of you!"

Andrew was quick to respond, "We're fine Grandpa. There's a roll bar on the back that stops the four-wheeler from flipping over."

"That's not a roll bar, Andrew! That's a rack to carry your gear."

"But it will stop the four-wheeler from flipping. It's never flipped."

"Andrew," Fred said, "I've been an engineer for forty-eight years, and I've learned a little bit about machines. Trust me on this. Had you stayed on the gas for about one more second, it would have flipped."

"You're sure?"

"Yeah, I'm sure. I want both of you to give me your word. No more wheelies. Nada. Zip. None. Do I have your word?" Reluctantly Eric and Andrew promised. Fred said, "Good, because if I ever see you doing a wheelie again, the four-wheelers go back to your dad's house. I won't be a part of your killing yourself by a dumb stunt if I can help it."

That seemed to stop the wheelies. Speed, however, was another thing. Twelve-year-olds are, in their minds, invincible. They simply assume they are in control, and nothing bad can happen. Fred began to realize that the boys stopped doing wheelies, not because they thought they might get killed, but because they knew he would follow through and take their four-wheelers. So he stopped preaching safety and tried to get them to see the possibility of losing their four-wheelers.

"You know," he said, "The faster you ride, the faster things will wear out or break, and the greater your chance of wrecking and breaking something expensive. I've heard your dad say he wasn't going to lay out big bucks to fix four-wheelers.

The boys knew all this was true, and it made sense to them. Apparently they were perfectly willing to risk breaking their necks, but not losing their four-wheelers. Fred makes it a point to run into them now and then on the hill to see how they are doing. They still allow their speed to creep up a little on occasion, but he hasn't observed the "edge of control" riding he saw earlier. I know there will still be times when they feel that urge for speed. It has been said, "The good Lord protects fools and Englishmen." There isn't much British blood in their ancestry, so I pray often that the old adage extends to twelve-year-olds until they get older and wiser.

The Crash

As a grandparent I relearned something I had forgotten after our sons were grown. No boy, as he is growing, can resist the temptation to run, jump, and see how high he can reach. Boy-size fingerprints work their way up the wall, over time, then from the top of the door to the ceiling. There are no known threats or punishments that will stop this behavior. It's just something every boy has to do.

Eric was spending a night with us last winter and asked me to take him by his house to pick up a movie he wanted to watch. As we pulled up to the house, I noticed the driveway was glazed over with ice. I cautioned Eric to walk carefully. I got the customary, "I know. I'm fine, Grandma." He picked his way carefully across the drive and into the house.

His return trip was a different story. He sprinted from the door, across the drive and leaped high in the air to touch the net of a basketball goal set up near the end of the driveway. As he came down, his feet flew out from under him, and he crashed to the ground with a loud thud. He lay absolutely motionless on the pavement. My mind raced. "Oh dear God, please let him be alive!" He was lying face down. Later it occurred to me that I probably should not have moved him, but I couldn't wait to answer the terrible question that filled my mind. Is he alive? I turned him over and there was still no movement. Terrified, I knew I needed help, and quickly. With shaking hands I called Fred, who was three blocks away, on my cell phone. "Come help me! Eric fell on the ice, and he isn't moving!" As I talked, Eric began to move, and by the time I hung up, he was sitting up, looking dazed. Fred arrived as I was struggling to get Eric to his feet. Clearly, he was unable to walk by himself, and it took both of us to get him to the car.

As we started for the hospital, Eric asked, "Where are we going?" Fred told him that he had been injured in an accident, and we were taking him to the hospital so he could be checked over to be sure he was okay. Immediately Eric became hysterical "No! I'm not going to the hospital! They will give me a shot." Our fears intensified. Eric had never been afraid of needles, even at an early age. His brother Andrew had been afraid of needles, but not Eric. This was not Eric talking, and we knew he was in trouble. We called his mother who was returning from a business meeting, and let him talk to her. By the time we arrived at the hospital, she had been able to calm him a little, and his sobbing slowed. The emergency room doctor examined and questioned him and sent him off to the X-ray department. Eric's first memory after leaping was when we walked with him down the hall to the emergency room. We gave a prayer of thanks as we were told that the scans the radiologists had done showed no evidence of a skull fracture or internal bleeding. He did have a concussion and the doctor told us to keep an eye on him for any change in behavior. By that time, Beth had arrived. We returned home, and she waited with Eric until the doctors released him.

Eric still has no memory of the fall. We, on the other hand, will never forget it. His brother Andrew has dedicated himself to making sure Eric never forgets his folly. When the air turns cold and ice freezes on the driveway, Andrew says, "Hey Eric, it's a great night for basketball!"

Bear Hunt

All the grandsons were gathered for leftovers Friday evening after Thanksgiving. The weather forecast was for falling temperatures, freezing rain changing to snow with one to three inches accumulation. Thus, it was inevitable that one of the guys would come up with, "I have a great idea! Let's go camping up at Buzzards Rock." Buzzards Rock is a thirty foot sheer rock face at the highest point on the hill behind our home. It has been explored by neighborhood children for generations.

This was, in fact, not a great idea, but a pretty dumb one, even for that crew. We have a long standing practice that if there is no significant risk of death or serious injury, or doesn't involve us in any way in the practice of feeding gerbils, we let kids learn from their own mistakes. I looked at Fred. He went off to consult with the parents. The forecast was for a low of 36°, so frostbite was unlikely, but the risk of hypothermia could be an issue. After some discussion, Fred returned and announced, "You can go, but with some conditions."

"Like what?"

"Condition number 1:"

"Yeah, we know. No women, no beer and no left-handed cigarettes." Fred knows this stopped being funny some time ago, but he just can't resist having them repeat it.

"Condition number 2: Under no circumstances are you to go on top of the rock or cross over the ridge."They raised their right hands and took the customary oath, which they would probably break, but at least they would be careful. No child of their ages believes he can be injured, but the boys were pretty sure any survivors would be severely punished in the event anything bad happens.

"Condition number 3: If you get wet, come down immediately. If one guy gets cold and leaves the hill, everybody comes down. Stay together. You have to promise me you will stay together no matter what."

"What's the big deal about that?"

"Well, that cavity in the rock where you guys go to stay dry might look pretty good to a bear or a bobcat looking to get out of this weather. Stash your food away from the camp and find some sturdy sticks you can use as spears. If you stand in a circle facing out, you have a better chance of fending off any bear who might want to take over your camp." The words *bear* and *chance* hung in the air for about sixty seconds. Finally someone got up the nerve to ask the question that was on everyone's mind.

"Ba- ba-bear? There are bears up there?"

"It doesn't happen often, but every now and then someone spots a set of tracks in the area." The nervous glances exchanged among the campers' ranks told me that Fred had hit on a perfect plan to insure the guys would, in fact, find some sturdy staffs and stay together. No supervision required. I know Fred isn't that smart. I'm sure he was reliving a childhood camping trip from sixty or so years ago. Obviously his long-term memory is more robust than the short-term variety.

Fred continued, "Condition number 4: Take two cell phones to call if you have any problems or need us to pick you up at the edge of the woods. Do you have flashlights with good batteries?"

"Yeah," they replied, "we have batteries. Why two cell phones?"

"In case the bear eats one."

Fred was on a roll now. At that instant, a rag-tag group of three twelve-year-old boys, one nine-year-old and a seven-year-old became transformed into a close-knit, if somewhat nervous, fighting unit. No bear with half a brain would willingly enter that camp. "Not me, man! I got a wife and kids. Let the bobcat do it."

Fred began to supervise the choice of clothing. "You aren't dressed nearly warmly enough, Andrew. Take lots of layers that you can put on when you get to the top."

"I'm fine."

"You are not fine. You will be colder up there than you ever imagined."

"I'm fine, Grandpa!"

Jake chimed in, "I'm burning up! I have way too many clothes on."

"You'll be the first to freeze, Jake. Let me put a tag on your toe so they'll know where to ship the body."

"I'm fine, Grandpa."

After some appropriate rolling of the eyes, Fred began loading boys and gear into the van. "Let's see. Sleeping bags, camp stove, matches, hotdogs, nacho chips, candy bars, water bottles, Hooters calendar and flashlights. It's all there." The freezing drizzle had already turned to snow when they arrived at the drop-off point around 5 p.m. The boys relayed gear up the mountain until about seven o'clock. The last trip was strictly by flashlight.

Fred returned to the house, and we started a pool, predicting how long the guys would last. I had 9:30 p.m. At 9:20, the phone rang.

"We're starting down. Jake is cold. Can you pick us up?"

When Fred arrived at the drop-off point, five shivering campers were already there. The descent, without gear, took ten minutes as opposed to the half hour they had taken to climb up. The only apparent casualty was one of the cell phones, which was miraculously recovered from the snow the next morning. Fred began the debriefing while the bodies were still cold and the memories crisp.

"What happened to the phone? Did the bear eat it.?"

"We slid down a big bank, and Zach's phone fell out of his pocket. It was dark, and we couldn't look for it."

"What happened to the flashlights?"

"The batteries went dead." Likely the result of checking out every sound in the night to make sure a hungry bear wasn't approaching the camp. There could, however be a connection with the Hooters calendar.

The debriefing went well.

"What did you do right?"

"We stayed together. We stored our food away from the camp. We kept our matches in a dry container."

"And what did you learn that might make your next trip better?"

"Spare batteries. Cooking frozen hotdogs takes a lot longer than you might think. Keep the cell phone in a zippered pocket. Don't take anyone along that might get cold."

"And that would include…?"

"All of us."

The cousins went home, and the twins would recruit a couple of friends to make two more attempts that winter. Their best time was 11:30 p.m. I asked Fred why he didn't go with them sometime for moral support.

"Are you kidding? Thirty years ago I got talked into taking Rich and Craig and two of their buddies winter camping out at the old Scout property. It got down to 10° that night. The boys were all talking about how warm they were in their sleeping bags. They lied. I promised God that if he let me live I would never go winter camping again. Besides, everyone knows there are bears up there!"

"What a Wuss!"

Victory

There is a tugging of the heart for young boys to explore the great outdoors. Why else would they repeatedly risk freezing, eat burned food cooked over an open fire and sleep on the hard ground? I suspect this compulsion is genetic and has been passed down through countless generations. Whether or not this is true, it is that desire for adventure that has sustained the Scouting program for decades. Eric and Andrew never joined the Boy Scouts, so they failed to learn the motto "Be Prepared" at an early age. That may be why they experienced several failed attempts at spending the night atop Buzzards Rock. Also, Fred hadn't helped their confidence much on their first trip when he suggested storing their food away from the camp to avoid attracting any hungry bears into their campsite. Actually, as I said previously, no bear with any sense at all would come within a mile of that crew. I guess it might be possible to attract an extremely dumb bear that was also hungry, but I think the chance of doing so is pretty remote.

Finally, at age thirteen, they decided a little preparation might be a good thing, and they began their one-night survival plan. Early March, just after a winter thaw, Eric, Andrew and five of their henchmen began planning another assault on Buzzards Rock. They started making lists of things they would need, as opposed to, "Hey, we still have a couple of hours of daylight left. Let's go camping up on Buzzards Rock!" The day before the assault, they gathered firewood and stashed it at the camp. The next day their four-wheelers made several trips to the top of the mountain shuttling sleeping bags, camp stools, water, a Coleman stove, cooking pots and pans, toilet paper, other assorted camping items, and of course, pepperoni buns, ingredients for S'mores , cookies, chips, sodas, two pounds of sausage and two pounds of deer burger. Hey, just because you are roughing it doesn't mean you can't eat well.

On the afternoon of D-Day, Eric, Andrew, Bobby, Cage, Dillon, Jacob and Wesley assaulted the mountain. We didn't hear from them until shortly after daybreak when we heard the sound of four-wheelers in the driveway. Fred went out to make sure there was no emergency. There was not, but some of the boys were ready for a warm bed. A few still hadn't embraced the "Be Prepared" concept, and they ended up on top of the mountain with seven boys and three sleeping bags, so those without sleeping bags spent most of the night sitting around the fire trying to keep warm.

There was a quick victory party over pancakes, eggs and juice. I conducted the customary debriefing. "Were you cold?"

Unanimous, "Yes ma'am."

"Did you cook anything?"

"We fought over your pepperoni buns until they were gone, then we got some snacks and made some S'mores. Then we got hungry, so we cooked the sausage and burger." I think they came back with one small package of Graham crackers. Apparently they had more crackers than chocolate or marshmallows.

"Did you see any bears?"

"No, but we could hear some coyotes howling and running around down below the rock. Dillon said he would kill them with his knife that had a six-inch blade" Now, there's a picture story.

"Yeah," chimed in Bobby. "He said he would kill them, but he wanted to send the little black kid down to check them out first!" After the laughter died down, Bobby launched into his version of what really happened. Each boy, in turn added his report where, not surprisingly, he became the real hero who had bravely saved the day for the others. Anyone who says teenagers are always non-communicative has never talked with a gang of thirteen-year-olds who have just returned from a successful camping trip.

"Did anything else exciting happen?"

"Yeah," said Andrew. "I thought I saw an enormous V-shaped spaceship. It made no noise and just glided slowly overhead."

"We told him it was just a flock of geese, and he was starting to see things, and that he needed to get some sleep." (Laughter all around)

"Well," countered Andrew, "It was dark and it really looked like a big UFO. We did see a shooting star though. That was cool. It was really bright and lit up the sky." Interestingly, none of the boys could remember seeing a meteorite entering the atmosphere before. I'm thinking it was nice that they could spend the night on top of that mountain looking up, instead of looking down at a video game. After a time, the stories died down, and one by one, the boys wandered off to bed to catch up on the sleep they had lost the night before. I'm sure their sleep was accompanied by sweet dreams of victory.

Then the work for the Expedition Support Team, yours truly, began – washing the smoky clothes and opening windows to air out the house. I guess that's a small enough price to pay for being a part of such a courageous adventure.

I'm Fine!

Teenagers clearly don't like to be told what to do. Most adult suggestions are met with "I'm fine!" No amount of debate will cause them to change their position until they discover for themselves that they are, in fact, not fine. Then they can reverse field with blazing speed.

Fred relates the following story:

The twins built a hunting blind up on the hill and were planning on sowing a food plot nearby to attract deer to the area. Eric asked if I would go with him to help measure the plot, so he could determine how much seed he needed to sow. I agreed, and we started up the street toward a trail which I estimated would be a fifteen minute climb to the blind.

Eric didn't want to take the trail through the open woods. He knew a shortcut that was better. So I said, "O.K." and let him take the lead. We turned left on another street, and when we arrived at the end of the pavement, I noticed Eric's shortcut took us through two hundred yards or so of tall grass and underbrush. I also noticed that instead of boots Eric was wearing shorts and tennis shoes.

"Eric," I suggested, "I don't think you should go that way in shorts and tennies. It looks like pretty good snake habitat to me. Let's go back and take the trail."

"I'm fine!"

"Eric, there are a lot of copperheads in the area this summer. If you want to go this way, let's at least go back to the house and get you some high boots and jeans."

"I'm fine, Grandpa!"

So I'm thinking: Copperhead bites are painful but seldom fatal, and we are ten minutes or so from the local hospital. Well, it's his party, so we press on.

We hadn't gone fifty yards when Eric almost ran over me heading back the way we had come. I heard "Snake!" as he flashed by.

"Where?" I asked.

"Up ahead, on that bush!"

I un-holstered a pistol I carry for such occasions and made my way slowly toward where Eric had been. There, sunning himself on the limb of a bush, was a small garter snake. Apparently Eric and the snake came eyeball to eyeball, and Eric blinked first. I shook the limb, and the little fellow disappeared into the underbrush.

"It's O.K. Eric. It was just a garter snake and he's gone. Let's go."

"No. If it's O.K. with you, Grandpa, let's take the trail through the woods."

"I think that's a great idea, Eric. You fine?"

"I'm fine, Grandpa."

Raccoon

Eric and Andrew sow grass for deer at their food plot up on the hill. They also have a corn feeder which looks like a bucket with a plastic rod and ball sticking out the bottom. The feeder hangs head-high, and when a deer bumps the ball with its head, a valve releases a small amount of corn.

Fred and I were recently sitting in a local Mexican restaurant with Andrew and his friend, Grant. While we were waiting for our food, Grant began to tell the story of the boys' attempt at refilling the feeder with corn the previous evening. As he got into the story, Grant leaned forward on the edge of his chair like an old sailor spinning a yarn.

Andrew and I hauled a big bag of corn up the hill with our four-wheelers. It was almost dark when we got there. We noticed the lid to the feeder was off. When I worked the valve on the bottom of the feeder only a few grains of corn came out, so we figured it was empty. But when I pushed up on the bottom of the feeder, it felt really heavy. I told Andrew I didn't think it was empty."

Andrew said, "The valve is probably jammed. I'll get it."

I climbed back on my four-wheeler, and Andrew got under the feeder in order to push up on the ball to free it. Just as Andrew was about to hit the ball upward with the heel of his hand, I saw a little leaf sticking over the top edge of the feeder. I was thinking the feeder must be heavy because it was full of wet leaves. Just then Andrew hit the ball upward with a real shot and launched this huge raccoon straight up in the air. As he went up, I noticed his ear looked a lot like a leaf. When he came back down and landed on the rack of my four-wheeler, I only noticed his teeth. He was not a happy camper! I thought he was going to attack me, but he bounced off the four-wheeler and landed on the ground. It was getting pretty dark and we couldn't see the raccoon, but we could hear him running around in the leaves. He didn't seem to be leaving, and we didn't think that was a good sign.

We fired up the four-wheelers and took off. We stopped after a couple of hundred yards, just long enough to agree we would fill the feeder another day when there was more daylight left. I think we might have made it off the hill in record time.

Great Indian Raid of 1973

To Zach, Jackson, Jacob and Eva,

If at some time in the future, your father criticizes you unduly about your mischievous behavior, as parents are prone to do from time to time, you may find it helpful to know about the Great Indian Raid of 1973. The Great Indian Raid took place when Rich was eight and Craig was six.

Sometime in the summer of 1973, your grandfather and I noticed that when we called Carol, our favorite babysitter, she never seemed to be available. We didn't think much about it the first couple of times, but the pattern continued. She had been a good dependable sitter, so we didn't want to replace her. Finally we decided she was about the age where boys and school activities complicate schedules, and we set out to find another sitter.

Many years later we learned the rest of the story. I was watching Aly at the community swimming pool and ran into Carol, now an adult woman who worked as an architectural designer. We sat by the pool with soft drinks, catching up on old times. After a while she said, "I have something to tell you from a long time ago. You would never guess what happened the last time I sat for you."

It seems soon after we left the house that evening for a movie, Rich and Craig made a proposal to her. "I bet we can tie you up and you can't get loose." Carol recalled how cute they were, and that she had given no serious thought to their actually being able to tie her that securely. In a reckless moment she took the challenge. What she didn't know was that Rich had taken a recent interest in an old Boy Scout manual, particularly the section on knots. The next two hours were pretty much a blur for Carol, who sat bound to a chair while the boys whooped and did a war dance around her, only stopping a couple of times to give her a drink of water. Her pleas for release were answered only by more whooping and dancing. Shortly before we returned home, the boys untied her, and all participants, for their own good reasons swore an oath of secrecy. Apparently Carol felt that after twenty-two years, the statute of limitations had run out.

So if Dad ever tells you that he would never have thought of behaving as badly as you, ask him about the Great Indian Raid of 1973.

TEENRAGERS

Top of the Menu

We have always believed in living somewhat frugally and not wasting resources that could be put to better use. We also tried to instill this concept in our children. When they were in their early teens, they had allowances and were making some of their own money. To help them learn the consequences of unnecessary spending, we had the following two rules for eating out, except for special occasions:

If you go to the top of the menu, you have to pay two dollars of your own money.

If you order a second drink, you have to pay for it.

They, of course, grumbled that this was unfair. The lesson took though. During college years, when we took them and their friends out to dinner, they enjoyed telling their friends about the two rules. Now they like to tell their children the rules in order to impress them with how tough they had it when they were kids, but I notice they have established similar rules.

Escape

If you find your grounded teen or pre-teen has escaped from his or her bedroom window after being sent to the bedroom for confinement, it may be the continuation of a tradition firmly established in our neighborhood by Jeannie Makris Cain over thirty years ago.

When Jeannie was upset with her parents, she would often attempt the "great window escape." Most of her escape attempts were spontaneous, but some involved detailed planning. A bag would be packed and hidden under the bushes in the back yard until darkness could conceal her exit. She never really made it very far. Mr. and Mrs. Makris would either capture her or watch quietly for Jeannie to have second thoughts about a lonely nighttime departure and return home. Often as not though, she would leave the bag under the bushes, just in case.

Jeannie's lack of complete success didn't discourage our sons, who were a few years younger and considered Jeannie to be daring and imaginative, as in, "Hey Craig, the bag is under the bushes again! Let's go find a spot where we can watch."

Rich made his first escape when he was ten or eleven. I had sent him to his room for some now-forgotten offense, and some time later I decided to check on him to see how he was doing. He was doing just fine. The window was open, the curtains flapping in the breeze and Rich was on the other side of the neighborhood playing football with his buddies. I don't remember details, but I'm sure I extended his sentence for unlawful flight to avoid prosecution.

Craig was the first, I believe, to extend the escape plan to a friend. Chip had asked his mom if he could go cruising with Craig in our old 79 Bronco. Wilda told Chip, "Nothing doing," and Chip decided to turn in early, which should have been a tip-off. Later in the evening, Wilda entered Chips room and, with a little sadness in her soul for having denied him, bent over his bed to give his cheek a good night kiss. What she kissed was the first pillow in a Chip-shaped pillow decoy. Feeling a breeze, she turned on the light to discover an open window and the top of a ladder still resting on the windowsill.

Thirty heartbeats later, the sadness had evaporated and Wilda was headed up the street in hot pursuit. It didn't take long to round up the usual suspects, and as she pulled alongside the Bronco she yelled, "Craig Goddard, do you have Chip in there?" Now, Craig is nothing if not polite when he is caught red handed in some escapade, and the greater the offense, the smoother he becomes. Needless to say, he was absolutely charming in this instance.

"Yes I do, Mrs. Fruner, and you don't have to worry. He's in good hands." Wilda knew Chip was anything but in good hands, so she demanded he ride home with her and yelled to Craig as she drove off, "Come by and get your ladder on your way home!"

To this day, when I drive by an open window in the neighborhood, I think fondly of Jeannie and the pioneering work she did for children's freedom over thirty years ago.

Sure!

Fourteen-year-old Beth returned home from visiting a nearby friend. She came in the front door and announced, "The reason I smell like smoke is, everyone was smoking over there." She quickly headed for a nearby bathroom, and we could hear the unmistakable sound of mouthwash being gargled. Her older brothers, who witnessed this, could not contain their laughter. They didn't buy the story any more than we had.

They are all in their forties now, and any questionable excuse is likely to be met with, "The reason I smell like smoke is ….."

The Inside Job

My parents took a trip to visit my brother in Scituate, Massachusetts. The second night they were gone, we got a call from their nearby neighbor who told us there was a strange car in Mom and Dad's driveway, and lights were on in the living room. She was concerned that someone might have broken into the house. She asked if we wanted her to go over and see what was going on. We told her, "Definitely not. That might be a risky thing to do." Fred called the Sheriff and arranged to meet him there. As he hung up the phone, he said, "Wait a minute. Do you have the key to your folks' house?"

I said, "Yes. It's in my purse."

He said, "Go take a look and see if it's still there." I did and there was no key.

He asked, "Where's Beth?" I could see where this was going and was pretty sure we had just called the Sheriff on our own daughter. A deputy was already at the house when we got there. He told us the house was locked and there was no sign of forced entry.

Fred said, "We're pretty sure it was an inside job. The key is gone from where my wife put it, and our daughter would be our first guess. We're sorry for all your trouble."

The deputy grinned and said, "No problem. Happens all the time. I'm just glad you weren't burglarized."

When Beth got home that evening, we told her about the incident. She asked, "Was anything taken?"

We told her, "We don't think so. The house was locked back up when we got there, and we didn't think to take the key to get in." We also told her that the Sheriff got a description of the car and a partial plate number from the neighbor. He was pretty sure he could get a match when their system was up in the morning. Beth went to bed looking a little worried.

The next morning we looked in the purse and the key was back. As Beth was eating breakfast, Fred said, "I haven't heard from the Sheriff. He's surely had enough time to make a positive I.D. by now. I think I'll give him a call."

As Fred was punching in the numbers, Beth said, "Hang up the phone, Dad. You already know it was me. Scott and I and some friends thought it would be cool to sneak in to Grandma's house and have a party when she was gone."

"Yes I do know who it was, Beth, and I want you to choose the punishment that fits the situation best." He handed her a prepared form with options to check.

1. *If she fesses up right away – Grounded for two weeks*
2. *If she stalls for a while to decide – Grounded for one month*
3. *If she really stonewalls – Grounded for two months*

Beth studied her options and asked quietly, "I guess it's too late to check Number 1?"

"I'm afraid so. I think you barely got in under option 2." Beth sighed and made her mark. It could have been worse. I suspect Fred didn't give her the maximum sentence because it was probably the kind of stunt he would have tried when he was her age.

Lectures

As children approach their teens they begin tuning out suggestions from parents and grandparents. When they are fifteen, pretty much all communication with adults stops. Aly had trouble remembering to fasten her seatbelt without being reminded. Repeated lectures on the importance of buckling up were ineffective, and being reminded when another teen was present embarrassed her. Finally, Fred said, "Look Al, I don't like lecturing you all the time, and you certainly don't like being lectured, but I'm not about to give up on this seatbelt thing. What do you say, we set up a code? The number 10 will be a signal to fasten your seatbelt. Do you think that's worth a try?"

Aly said, "Sure." It worked like a charm. Sometimes she would remember on her own. When she didn't, a "10" code would be quickly implemented. When one of her friends asked what 10 meant, she explained that it meant that she was supposed to fasten her seatbelt. Sure, she was still being corrected by an adult, but now it was a game and she was a part of it. She stopped tuning

Fred out, and over time, she learned to remember her seatbelt without being reminded.

When the boys approached the teen years, we found them equally forgetful and harder-headed as well. So the list was expanded over time to Ancient Granfodder's Lectures for Grasshopper, Sidewinder, Weedhopper, Scorpion and Bear (Fred's nicknames for the boys). It became a game to remember what 8 or 25 represented, and most of their friends thought it was kind of cool. It's been a few years since the lectures were published, and the novelty has worn off somewhat, but a framed copy still hangs on their bedroom walls. When they are asked to consult the list, sometimes they do – sometimes they don't. Fred says, "That's okay. At least they know how I feel about those things, and they haven't taken the list down from the wall."

Ancient Granfodder's Lectures for Grasshopper, Sidewinder, Weedhopper, Scorpion and Bear

1. Key to Life: Love all that is good, and look after each other, especially those who could use a break.

2. Watch your back cast! We're all in this boat together, and it's smaller than you think.

3. "You can't roller skate in a buffalo herd, but you can be happy if you've a mind to."

— *Roger Miller*

4. Life is a gift. Don't forget to unwrap it and say, "Thank you."

6. If you mess up, fess up and get on with it. A little embarrassment is a small price to keep your name as an honest man.

8. Learn mental toughness. Focus on your goal. Don't let a bad play, bad call or a negative comment from a teammate, opponent or coach distract you from concentrating on your next play.

10. Buckle your seatbelt, Moron!

12. Avoid doh-rugs like poison. They are!

25. If you have something important to attend, plan to arrive at least ten minutes early, then if the unexpected happens you're still on time.

37. A part of maturity is learning to organize your time and stuff to accomplish the things you want to do.

42. Only a loser tries to blame his lack of performance on someone else. We've got a $5 fine for whining.

50. If you think I've skipped some lectures, you're right.

51. If you are not sure what is the right thing to do, go back to lecture no. 1 and think about it really hard. It will come to you.

Counting Cheerleaders

Since Aly joined the cheerleading squad, our home has become *Hotel Central* for the team. Any weekend night, we may have at least two or three girls for the night, often six or eight. I think our record was thirteen for spaghetti one evening after practice. Let's see, there are Aly, Becca, Maddie, Shanna, Rebecca, the two Emily's, Courtney, Morgan, Holly, Ashton, Kala, Kourtney, Lakyn and Eliza. That's fifteen. Two must be missing. They didn't spend the night though – just there for a fill up. The girls are expected to make themselves at home, so at any given time, there may be girls in the kitchen, family room, online in the office or in Aly's room. When I would ask Fred how many girls were there, he would always reply, "Six", "Nine"…or whatever the number might be. It puzzled me that even though the girls were scattered all over the house, he always seemed to know exactly how many girls were there. "How do you do that?" I asked."

"Simple. I count the number of flip flops in the entry and divide by two." I tried his system, and it worked like a charm, until one night I counted seven. I think he may have hidden one just to mess with my mind.

Grandpuppies

Fred loves it when the cheerleaders visit. They call him Grandfather, and he calls them Grandpuppies. It must be a male thing. I notice fourteen-year-old Eric and Andrew are always available on those nights also. "Can I stay, Nan? I'll go to bed on time and not mess anything up."

We got to the term *Grandpuppies* shortly after Fred began calling me Poochie. When our neighbor Julie heard this for the first time, she questioned, "Poochie?"

"Yeah," Fred explained, "That's what I call her when she's nice."

Julie bit. "What do you call her when she's not nice? Oh…never mind."

He'd better never! Anyhow, I asked him, "If I am Poochie, what does that make you?"

"I dunno. The Old Dog, I guess." Fred thinks anything worth doing is worth overdoing, so he continued the canine theme. When Beth would call for me, he would announce, "It's your puppy, Poochie." Naturally Aly became Grandpuppy, and when her friends started calling Fred Grandfather, they became Grandpuppies too. And that's the story of how our whole family went to the dogs in a few short weeks.

Foul Shooting

To say the basketball goal in our driveway is overused is a gross understatement. The court is a little small for five-man teams, but three on three is pretty common. There are floodlights, so the game often lasts until Fred enforces the 11:00 p.m. curfew and turns out the lights. The twins could be doing a lot worse things than playing a pickup basketball game with their friends, so we don't discourage their inviting a gang of their buddies over for a game.

There is one little problem, however, we have been unable to solve:

CLEANUP! - More accurately, the lack thereof. Despite cajoling, repeated reminders and threats, soda cans and water bottles continue to line the top of the garden wall. Basketballs, candy wrappers, tee shirts, hoodies, hockey sticks (hockey sticks?), ball caps and an occasional cell phone have to be retrieved the next morning. One morning Fred had to pry a basketball from under the car and clean up the shrapnel one too many times The next time the gang showed up to play, he called a team meeting.

"What's up with the trashing of my driveway? I must have reminded you guys a hundred times, and you still leave the place a mess!"

"We just forget, Grandpa. Sometimes we go off for a snack or something to drink after the game, and we forget to come back and clean up."

"Well, I'm going to help you remember. I'm tired of reminding you. Starting today, any time I have to clean up your mess, I will confiscate one basketball. If you run out of basketballs, you will have to earn them back by doing chores or extra cleanup." The boys knew how bad the situation had become, so they accepted the decision with only some minor grumbling.

The team had five basketballs when the cleanup campaign began. I think they would be hard-pressed to say which basketball belonged to which boy, although they claim otherwise. After three months, Fred had collected seven basketballs, and the boys still had two. The expanded number of basketballs remains unexplained, and Fred isn't sure he even wants to know where they came from. The guys are doing a little better since they have been down to two basketballs, but Fred still has a recurring nightmare about having to build a basketball storage room onto the house.

Personally, I think we can hang on until the boys graduate and go off to college, but I wouldn't bet the farm on it.

The Sooner the Better

Eric and Andrew were invited to a party by classmates Emily and Erin, who are also twins. When we dropped the boys off at about 7:20 p.m. Tom, the girls' father, was on the porch. Rolling down the car window, I called, "When should we pick them up?"

Without hesitation, Tom answered, "7:30 would be good." Then, he smiled and said, "No, the party should be finished a little after 9:00."

Fred and I both laughed because of the quickness of his answer, and we knew that as the father of two teen-age daughters, he was only half-kidding about 7:30.

We're Allowed to…

When Susan and Matt, our niece and nephew were younger, my mother went to stay with them while their parents vacationed in The Bahamas. Mom was always a kind and caring person, sometimes to a fault. She was always careful not to upset any of her grandchildren with little things like rules and regulations, for fear they might not care for her. It was also inconceivable to her that any of the little darlings might not be completely honest with her. So when underage Susan told her that she was allowed to drive the car around the block if she was careful, Mom let her do it. Matt added to the *we're allowed to do that* theme by declaring that he was allowed to wear shorts any time he

wanted. He added that they were allowed to eat chocolates before meals, as long as it wasn't too many. It was January in Boston, and the milk chocolates were disappearing rapidly, but Mom bought it.

Steve and Caroline returned from their vacation. Mom, who was always too honest, said, "I was surprised that you allow Susan to drive the car." She added, "Matt hasn't had warm clothes on since you walked out the door. He told me he was allowed to wear shorts any time."

Needless to say, all the participants were in big trouble. Susan and Matt are now grown, with small children of their own. I'm sure that any day now, they will be properly repaid by the Mother's curse.

"I hope you grow up and have children just like you!

You always were my favorite.

BIG KIDS

Gone Fishing

Grandfather Fred loves fishing. More specifically, he loves fishing the bays behind Ocean City. We've been going there since 1963, and our fishing has progressed from fishing from the Route 50 bridge and the bulkheads around 28th Street (an area now covered by condos) to rental boats out of Bahia Marina, to a little tri-hull and finally to our more seaworthy Bayliner, which by the way, I insisted he buy a few years before retirement. Fred loves telling his buddies that his wife made him buy a boat. Of course they never believe him.

Fred will fish through storms, rain, heat, cold and nothing biting. He loves the bay and knows just about every channel and current and hole as you can learn only from fishing the same waters for forty plus years. I, on the other hand, love fishing a little, if the weather is good and the fish are cooperative. A couple of hours and I'm ready to head back to shore.

I think my aversion to long fishing outings began when our children were small and we would pack them all into the car for a trip to some freshwater lake and fish from an aluminum john-boat. You can talk about heavy metal, but you have never really experienced sound until you have fished from an aluminum john-boat with a three, five and seven-year-old. Disregarding all logic, Fred demanded quiet and that the children keep their feet still in the boat. He got neither. We caught a few juvenile bass over the years, probably attracted by the noise made by their human counterparts, but there was always a dropped oar, spilled tackle box or feet kicked by a child bored out of his skull, and no self-respecting bass would come within a half mile of that boat. Fred is nothing if not fiercely stubborn, and it took him about ten years to get rid of that gong of a boat. Actually, I think we outgrew it, or he would probably still be out in the middle of some lake yelling, "Quiet!" Go figure.

Fred has mellowed somewhat since then, and he no longer expects children to be quiet. Imagine that! His only rule these days is "Under no condition will we leave the dock when the children in the boat outnumber the adults." I've been there, and I have to support him on that one.

Grandma's Noodles

Great grandmother Pearl Mabel Bleuer Goddard – her grandparents came to this country from a small village near Bern, Switzerland in 1852. Our children may have inherited their love of cheese, salami and noodles from her. She lived and died before most of our grandchildren were born, but my memories of her are still vivid. If you visited her home in the country – family, neighbor, door-to-door salesman – no matter, you couldn't leave without something to eat. More often than not, a plate of cheese and salami or trail bologna was offered.

Most Sundays you would find a large pot of steaming noodles on her kitchen stove, not the store-bought kind, but all homemade. Chicken was slowly simmered to make the broth for the noodles. When I visit her grave, I often think of her in heaven teaching someone how to make noodles. She was trained in home economics in college and taught in public schools. However, I think most of her recipes were handed down. So if you would ever like to make great noodles the hard way, here's how:

Beat two eggs. Add one teaspoon of salt. Add two cups of flour and just a little water to make the mixture stay together nicely. Knead just enough to mix. Not too much or the noodles will be tough. Place the ball of dough on a floured surface and roll with a large rolling pin to the desired thickness. Fold over the rolled out dough to make four layers, dusting each layer with flour so the layers don't stick together. Slice noodles to the desired width. Two inch squares makes "Jack straps." Cook in the broth just until they are not doughy. It's better to undercook them since the noodles will continue to cook in the broth after you remove them from the heat.

If this sounds like too much work, go to the store and buy some noodles, but remember to cook a chicken for the broth. Grandmother will be smiling down at you just for trying.

Toninni

Bill Toninni was a great umpire. Like any umpire, his eyesight might be challenged by a fan from time to time, but his spirit never was. His energy and showmanship added excitement to local high school and Little League baseball games. In the absence of a pregame show by ESPN or ABC, Bill would sometimes kick off a game with his own little pregame ceremony. After the pitcher was warmed up, and the catcher threw down to second base, Bill would dust off the plate. Then he would turn to the group of mothers who always sat directly behind home plate to keep an eye on Bill's ball and strike calls. He would smile and ask softly, "Ready ladies?"

The response in unison was, "Ready Bill."

Then singling out one enthusiastic mother, he would ask, "Ready Nina?"

"Ready Bill."

Toninni would then don his mask, turn back to the field with one fist raised high and roar, "PLAY BALL!" And the game was on.

Bill and Eleanor

We were in our twenties when Fred took a job at a pigments plant in Huntington, West Virginia. The new job offered increased responsibilities, but also entailed some additional risk. This, coupled with our lack of knowledge of the neighborhoods prompted our decision to rent for a while before buying a house. We had a four-year-old and a two-year-old boy and a small beagle. A quick glance at me would reveal that a third child was well on the way. House hunting was a discouraging experience. We quickly learned that renting a house is difficult when you have small children and a dog. Worse yet, the children seemed to be much more of a problem than the dog. After several rejections, I cried to Fred, "We can rent a house with the dog, but we will probably have to get rid of the children!"

We finally found a nice brick home in East Pea Ridge, a friendly neighborhood with wall-to-wall children. The moving van had just left and we were beginning to arrange our furniture when the doorbell rang. Standing at the door was a smiling older man who extended his hand and said, "I'm Bill Key. My wife Eleanor and I live two doors down the street. You will notice we have a fence all the way around the yard. The fence is designed to keep children and dogs in and not out. I just want you to know that you all are welcome at our house anytime."

We were overwhelmed by this act of kindness by a perfect stranger, but Bill and Eleanor were not to be strangers for long. Bill was a retired international union representative and Fred was in his first management position, and the two of them often enjoyed discussing the ins and outs of labor relations over a round of golf. In the two years that we lived in the neighborhood, Bill and Eleanor taught us an important life-lesson. The number of years you have lived does not have a whole lot to do with how old you are. The Keys were always among the first to arrive and the last to leave any neighborhood party. Any kindness that was shown to them would be promptly returned with interest. They were enthusiastic, well-read and were always interested in learning something new. Despite the difference in our ages, we found them fun to be around, and exchanged many visits.

It was during one of those visits that Bill told us what was to become one of our favorite stories, one that was to have increased meaning as the years have passed. Bill and Eleanor shared a cabin with another couple for a week each year. It was a one-room cabin, and when they wanted to change clothes, they would hang a sheet over a clothesline running through the center of the cabin. As the years passed, hanging up the sheet and taking it down became more of a hassle. Finally, everyone agreed just to take off their glasses.

Some years after we relocated again, we went back to visit. Bill and Eleanor were well into their eighties the last time we were there. They had both suffered some serious medical problems, but we found their enthusiasm for life undiminished. They are both gone now. We aren't sure how they died, but we are certain they died young.

The Ute

One September, during that brief period of serenity that falls between dealing with children and grandchildren, we took a wonderful trip with Craig and Gina to Ireland. The scenery was beautiful, and when we arrived at Killarney, County Kerry, we decided to take a ride in a horse-drawn jaunting car to explore the nearby roads and mountains. We were barely outside the Bed & Breakfast the next morning when we came upon Martin, a driver who offered us his services. He was very friendly, and his prices were better than those we had seen in the guidebook, so we hopped aboard.

After a few minutes in the jaunting car, we began to suspect why Martin's rates were so low. Martin had clearly been in the Irish whiskey for breakfast.

He would ignore traffic and turn completely around in his seat while driving in order to spin one yarn after another. Luckily, the horse had taken this trip so many times he knew the way and how to negotiate the intersections and light traffic. As we continued the tour, it became clear that the horse was running the show, and Martin's participation was entirely optional. Martin's heavy brogue was amplified by the whiskey, and it was difficult to follow his stories completely, but a common theme seemed to be the "Ute." "The trouble with the country is the Ute. The Ute don't understand anything. The Ute show no respect."

I knew the Ute were a well known Indian tribe in North America, but I had never heard of their presence in Ireland. Finally, I had to ask, "Who is this group that causes all the problems in Ireland?"

Martin growled impatiently at my lack of understanding. "The Ute! The Ute! You know...Teeenagers!"

Thus, "The trouble is the Ute" made our family's Classic Quote list, along with:

"Shut up and eat your pancakes."

"The reason I smell like smoke is…." and, "I tan't! I just tan't!"

What Mind?

I was bringing Fred's Aunt Louise home from her doctor's appointment. She asked, "When is my next appointment?" I told her the appointment was May 12.

"And how am I going to get there?"

"I will take you, Aunt Louise."

Well into her nineties, Aunt Louise was beginning to have some short-term memory loss. When she asked, "When is my next appointment, and how will I get there?" for the fifth time, the question was beginning to get to me.

"Aunt Louise, your next appointment is May 12. I will remind you when it is, and I will get you there on time. You don't have to worry any more about it. Just get it out of your mind."

Her reply was quick and to the point. "I don't have a mind, thank you! I used to have a mind, but now I no longer have one, so there is nothing to get it out of."

I just kept driving.

Norman

Norman and Jade became regular visitors at our home. Norman was a Jack Russell Terrier, and Jade was a Benji-type terrier that played straight man to Norman's antics. I made the mistake of giving them a treat one morning. Consequently, they would show up at our front door between 9:30 and 10:00 every morning. They never barked, but would be there patiently waiting for their snack when I opened the door. The doorbell rang one morning, and when I opened the door, there sat Norman and Jade in classic begging position. I found myself actually wondering for a second which of them rang the doorbell, until a familiar snicker originating behind a nearby shrub told me Fred had set me up. All the neighborhood kids loved the dogs. Norman was an excellent soccer player. There were no goals. Norman kept score by the length of time he could keep the ball away from a pack of ten-year-olds.

One day Russell, a bricklayer who had been working on our house addition, was sitting by the side of the driveway eating his lunch. We learned that he also bred Jack Russells. He said, "They are really great dogs." Bob, our next-door neighbor, was not entirely convinced.

"That may be so, but I wish they would stay home. I'm sure those two have been watering down the flowers in my flowerbed."

"Just ask him to stop," suggested Russell. "They're very intelligent." Then as a matter of demonstration, Russell said, "Norman, I left my glove over under that tree. Would you go fetch my glove?" If Russell pointed or used any other visual signals, they were well concealed. Norman trotted over, picked up the glove, brought it to Russell and started a game of tug of war over the glove. Bob, along with the rest of us, was astounded.

"Well," said Bob. "Any critter that is that smart, we'd better keep him around." Bob and Norman became great friends over the next few weeks. Later that summer three days went by and we hadn't seen Norman and Jade. We asked Bob if they had been by his house. He said, "No. I heard one of the neighbors complained about the dogs, and the owners gave Norman and Jade to someone who lived on a farm where they had plenty of room to roam".

The neighborhood children, as well as most of the adults were saddened by the dogs leaving. Norman and Jade were characters. Our neighborhood can be a little sleepy and ho-hum. It needed a couple of characters to add a little color. Eric and Andrew consoled themselves. At least Norman and Jade could run free, but they doubted if Norman would be able to find enough kids to get up a good soccer game.

Cousin Laura

All children need a Cousin Laura to visit. Laura has everything a young boy needs for a day of fun. She and her husband Bob live on farm bordering a small creek that runs clear most of the time. The creek holds bass, catfish, bluegill and a variety of other fish, as well as a few frogs and turtles.

Eric and Andrew, often accompanied by friends and visiting cousins, have spent hours along the creek fishing and hunting snakes and skipping rocks. On the ride home, I often hear the testimonial, "That was the most fun I've ever had!" On a summer day, a suggestion that it might be a nice day to visit the farm is all that is needed to produce a van load of boys with fishing rods.

Laura is a dedicated animal lover. She has two horses, four Jerusalem Donkeys, one dog, a couple dozen cats who roam the fields and a few pet chickens. All have names, excellent lifetime healthcare, and a brick or small stone to mark their burial spot when they leave this world. She has only one cat of her own. The rest have been dropped off by someone who knows she will feed and care for them, which she always does. Also, a bit of food is usually left down by the creek for raccoons that might be looking for a late night snack. True stewards, Laura and Bob were green long before green was cool.

Pity Party

I went into the garage and found Fred just standing and staring at his wall rack and peg board. He was mumbling under his breath, "I used to have a rake and a shovel and hammers and screwdrivers and even a measuring tape. What do I have now? Grandchildren!"

What a whiner! It isn't like I have a full set of spoons or knives. Not to mention, I haven't seen my cell phone in three days.

My Favorite

Nana Ruby, my mother, lived to the age of eighty-four. At a young age, she waited for a husband to come back from World War II. She had buried two children, a son at ten and a daughter at thirty-six. She tended to worry about a lot of small things, but when real tragedy struck, her faith carried her through. I was always amazed at how she could suffer such losses and still not lose her love of life. I think her strategy was to love those friends and family she still had even more. She had eleven grandchildren and sixteen great-grandchildren. At one time or another she told each one of them that he or she was always her favorite.

At the end of her funeral service, when the invitation was extended to friends and family to share memories, each grandchild who spoke related, "I was always her favorite. I know, because she told me so." After the second speaker, the congregation began to see the pattern and would chuckle approvingly or applaud each grandchild's claim. Those who knew her knew that she had not lied. Each and every grandchild was in fact her favorite.

Undercover

We had written about 90 percent of the stories for this book when my mother became seriously ill. She stayed with us until the time of her death. Then, all the activity involved with settling her estate added to an already busy schedule. As a result, it was about a year before we were able to work on the book again. We still had many stories to write, proofread and organize into chapters. We resolved to work several hours on the book every day. That just didn't happen. Writing a book requires a lot of concentration and periods of uninterrupted time, so we found it difficult to stick to our plan. The phone or doorbell would ring about every fifteen minutes, or so it seemed. There would be a telemarketer, charity, grandchild, friend, extended family member, friend of a friend, or a complete stranger wanting to sell us something, get a donation, have something fixed, or just wanting to chat. Also, when I am home, I am continually thinking of something that needs to be done around the house.

We realized we would have to get out of Dodge if we were going to make any progress. We packed tablets, files and the laptop into our camper and headed off for a quiet campground in Amish country. It was an unqualified success. There was no phone, little traffic noise, and not a soul who knew us.

We made more progress in one weekend than we had made in the last two months.

When we decided to make another trip, Eric saw us preparing the camper, and asked, "Where are you going, Grandpa?"

"We're going to Sugarcreek to work on our book, in peace and quiet."

"Can I come along?"

"No. You have to go to school. Besides you are one of the people we are hiding from."

I told Fred, "That was an awful thing to tell him," but Eric was un-fazed. Obviously, he had been hidden from before and had grown comfortable with the idea.

This Is Different

As the number of grandchildren grew, Fred established the following rule: Never leave the dock when the number of children exceeds the number of adults in the boat. However, we usually have two or three grandchildren along on any trip. When Fred resets the boat for another drift, if there are no boats nearby, he will let one of the kids steer for a few hundred yards. This starts when the grandchild gets old enough to sit on his lap and hold the wheel. One day when four-year-old Eva had taken the wheel, Beth began grumbling from the back of the boat. "What's the deal here? I wasn't allowed to run the boat until I was nearly thirty. You've really mellowed, Dad. Why are you Mr. Nice Guy now?"

Fred just grinned. "I'm old and trying to get into heaven now. Besides, I like Eva."

Concurrent Sentences

Fred tells people we have been married ninety-eight years, but we aren't sure it's going to last. When they look at him and wonder if he has lost his mind, he explains, "Forty-nine for her and forty-nine for me. That's a total of ninety-eight years. It's just like serving concurrent sentences." Many days, I must agree.

When a young couple announces they plan to be married, Fred always gives them the following pep talk. It isn't original with us, but we have been using it for so long I don't know who we should give credit for it:

"Of all our families and all our friends, pretty much all the people we know, our marriage is by far the most successful, and we're miserable half the time." When the couple turns to me for hope, I am just sitting there nodding my head in affirmation. Then we let them off the hook by telling them we also believe people who are alone are miserable a lot more than that. Also, the times when we aren't miserable can be pretty darn good. The point is that there are a lot of things that get in the way of maintaining a great relationship, but those things can be overcome if you are both willing to work hard enough at it.

When our children announced their engagements, we gave them a similar, but a little more personalized speech: "Congratulations. It is a brave and wonderful thing that you are about to embark on a journey, which at best, has a 50 percent chance of success. We want to wish you the best of luck and happiness, but if it doesn't work out, don't bring the children home for us to raise." They smile because they know if it became necessary, we would be there, but so far we have made it stick. It's all a matter of managing expectations.

Feng Shui

A senior couple, who shall remain nameless in order to protect the guilty, used Feng Shui to un-clutter their home.

They related, "We got rid of a lot of junk. We read that a principle involved in using Feng Shui to un-clutter a home is *If it doesn't give you pleasure, get rid of it.* Now, some days we just sit and stare at each other for hours."

Picture Memories

I stated in the first story of this book that my love of a bargain is legendary. Possibly this is exceeded only by my love of showing family pictures, more specifically pictures of grandchildren.

We were enjoying one of the best breakfasts in town at Quinet's Restaurant. The bacon, eggs and toast from thickly sliced home-made bread had been conquered. We were working on the last of the coffee when John motioned for me to come over to his table and said, "Carolyn, come over here. I have something to show you." John is a successful businessman and lawyer who was blessed with grandchildren a little later in life than most. I had heard that a new grandchild had arrived recently, so I was pretty sure what was up.

Strangely, John seemed to be looking behind me as I approached his table. Later I was to learn that Fred, still seated at our booth, was waving his arms at John and mouthing the words *No, don't do it.* When I got to the table John produced two pictures of his grandchildren and proudly showed them to me. They were beautiful and I told him so. As he was putting the pictures back in his wallet, I held out my folding photo-sleeves at shoulder height and they unfolded reaching nearly to the floor.

John realized his mistake, but it was too late. I saw a bit of color drain from his face, but he was the perfect gentleman and looked patiently at all the pictures, saying all the right things. Fred joined us and John said, "I only wanted to show her a couple of pictures of my grandchildren."

Fred was sympathetic. "I tried to warn you, John. She is undefeated and un-tied at this event."

To this day, John will tell his friends "Don't ever try to show Carolyn pictures of your grandchildren unless you have a whole morning to spend."

I plead guilty as charged. In this book I have attempted to show you some stories that picture the spirit of a child. They have been stored in my heart — my attic, if you will. Now it is your turn. The final section of this book, titled MY ATTIC, is a journal with lined pages where you can record some of the wonderful pictures that have been stored in your attic. And I promise that if you ever come to my house, I will be genuinely happy to look at them with you.

I ask only one thing of you. As you write your stories, be mindful that the spirits of many children have been darkened by threatening circumstances, in developed as well as developing countries.

The good news is we live in exciting times. For the first time in history, we have the communications, the technology and the resources to identify and solve world-wide problems that plague children. Let's do it. We just need the will to make it a priority. If you would like to learn more, the APPENDIX contains some useful information.

If you bought this book, clearly you love children and you probably already support one or more of these efforts. Keep up the good work and don't be hesitant to ask your friends and associates to join you. Compassion is contagious.

God bless you, and may you hear the laughter of a child every day of your life.

Got Kitty (Aly)

THEN

A Jackson Sandwich (Andrew, Jackson & Eric)

What? (Zach)

Yesss! (Jackson)

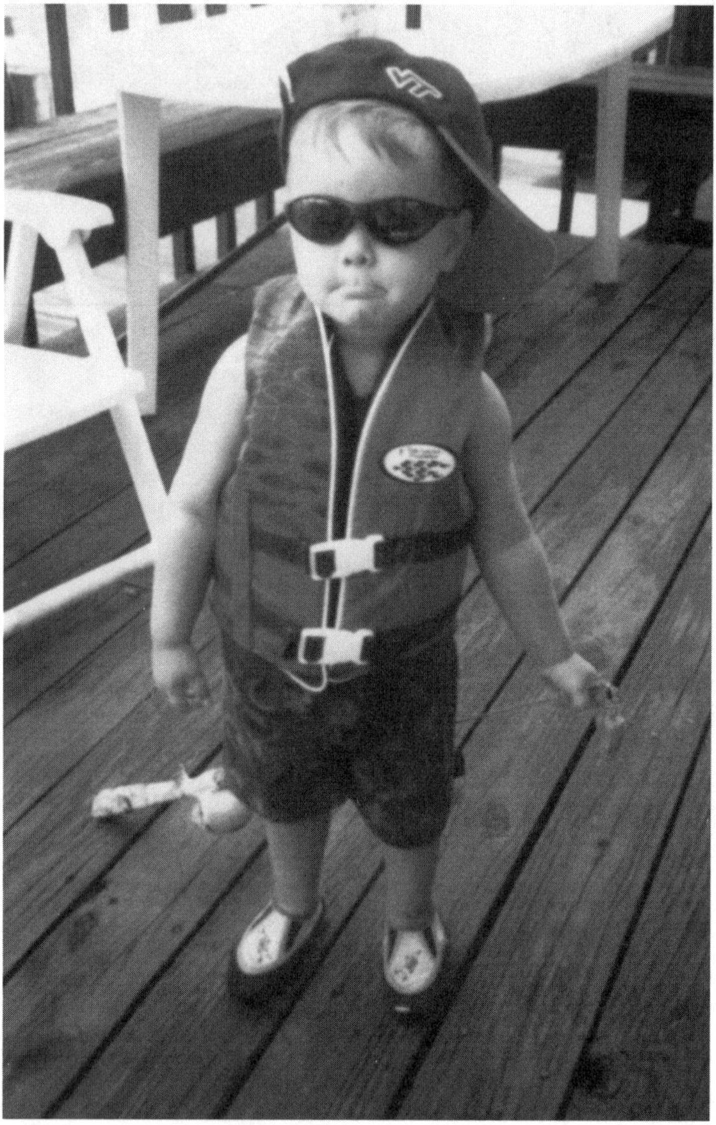

Anticipation (Jacob)

There's Another Flag (Eva)

Christmas 2011

NOW

MY ATTIC

THIS ATTIC BELONGS TO:

____

This is your attic. There are no rules or limitations. Fill it with stories or pictures of your kids, birds you have spotted, trips you have taken, or gerbils you have owned. You can fill it with anything you like. After all, it is your attic.

NANNY'S ATTIC

NANNY'S ATTIC

NANNY'S ATTIC

NANNY'S ATTIC

Carolyn Goddard

Carolyn Goddard

Carolyn Goddard

NANNY'S ATTIC

APPENDIX

Some Good News

UNICEF and the World Health Organization reported recently that significant progress is being made in reducing under-five child mortality rates. The child mortality rate has dropped 35% since 1990. The number of under-five deaths worldwide has declined from 12 million in 1990 to 7.6 million in 2010. Even so, improvements in child mortality rates will not be enough to meet the United Nations Goal set in 2000 to reduce child mortality rates by two-thirds by 2015, and the groups say more money is needed. Dr. Margaret Chan, director general of the World Health Organization, said in a statement, "This is proof that investing in children's health is money well spent, and a sign that we need to accelerate the investment through the coming years." She said many factors are contributing to reductions in child mortality, including better access to healthcare for newborns, prevention and treatment of childhood diseases, access to vaccines, clean water and better nutrition.

This is bittersweet news. The 7.6 million children that did die, is almost equal to the population of the city of New York. The good news is that we know we can significantly reduce the deaths, and the rate of decline is increasing. Again, it's a matter of priorities.

Similar gains are being made in other areas impacting child health. Goals for reducing by half the proportion of people without access to safe drinking water and improved sanitation have seen mixed results. The safe drinking water project is on pace to meet or exceed the goal. Sanitation is another story. Projections show that, at the current pace of reductions, the goal will be missed by 1 billion people, leaving 2.4 billion people without access to improved sanitation. Also, these are estimates. Accurate measurements are lacking in many areas. Even so, the goals do much to bring attention to significant problems and attract funding to reach these goals, and best practices have been identified that will positively impact further progress.

Much Still to be Done

Obviously the need in developing countries is great, but it is also not difficult to find children who need your help in your own state, and likely, your own neighborhood. Even in middle-class neighborhoods where poverty and poor nutrition are not problems, there are all too many children nearing adulthood who lack direction and the values needed to pursue a productive and rewarding life. They are well fed, but their spirits are undernourished. A lack of purpose causes many drift into counterproductive or self-destructive behavior.

The point is that problems that dim the spirit of a child come in many shapes and sizes. Pick a cause that speaks to you and be intentional about supporting it regularly with your time or money, or both. What you do will make a difference.

Three of my favorites:

The Rotary Foundation: The mission of The Rotary Foundation is to enable 1.2 million Rotarians, in 33,000 clubs and two hundred countries to advance world understanding, goodwill and peace through improvement of health, the support of education, and the alleviation of poverty. The Foundation is a not-for-profit corporation supported solely by voluntary contributions from Rotarians and friends of the Foundation who share its vision of a better world.

Areas of focus are peace and conflict resolution, disease prevention and treatment, water and sanitation, maternal and child health, education and literacy, economic and community development.

In 1985 Rotary launched its first worldwide project, Polio Plus, the first and largest internationally coordinated private-sector support of a public health initiative, with a pledge of $120 million. By 1988 Rotary had raised $247 million.

Inspired in part by Rotary's initiative, the World Health Assembly passed a resolution to eradicate polio, paving the way for the formation of the Global Eradication Initiative (GPEI). Since 1988, The Global Polio Eradication Initiative spearheaded by the World Health Organization, Rotary International, the US Centers for Disease Control and Prevention and UNICEF has achieved a 99% reduction in the number of polio cases worldwide, preventing 5 million cases of paralysis and 250,000 deaths.

Tackling the last 1% of polio cases is proving to be difficult and costly. Finishing the job is critical. The GPEI estimates the net economic benefit of eradication to be at least $40-50 million if transmission of wild polio viruses is interrupted by 2015, and going back to routine immunization would lead to an estimated four million paralyzed children over the next 20 years.

UMCOR: The United Methodist Committee on Relief (UMCOR) is a prominent worldwide humanitarian relief and development organization. It is a nonprofit agency of the United Methodist church. UMCOR provides relief in five core areas: Hunger, Health, Refugees, Emergencies and Relief Supplies. UMCOR is working in over 80 countries, including the United States. Its stated mission is to alleviate human suffering –whether caused by war, conflict, or natural disaster, with open hearts and minds to all people.

UMCOR is structured so that 100% of all donations go directly to the intended projects. All overhead, administrative and operating costs are covered by One Great Hour of Sharing, an annual collection taken at United Methodist Churches around the world in March.

Child Fund International, formerly Christian Children's Fund and China's Children Fund is an international child sponsorship group based in Richmond, Virginia, United States. The organization's stated mission is to help deprived, excluded and vulnerable children living in poverty have the capacity to become young adults, parents and leaders who bring lasting and positive change to their communities; and to promote societies whose individuals and institutions participate in valuing, protecting and advancing the worth and rights of children.

Child Fund was founded in 1938 as China's Children Fund by Presbyterian Minister, Dr. J. Calvitt Clarke to aid Chinese children displaced by the second Sino-Japanese War. The "child sponsorship" development concept used today stemmed from Clarke's early vision: one sponsor donates one amount to help one child.

Child Fund International works in 31 countries, including the United States, assisting 15.2 million children and their family members, regardless of race, creed or gender.

Some useful websites:

www.rotary.org — *The Rotary Foundation*

www.umcor.org — *UMCOR*

www.childfund.org — *Child Fund International*

www.drugfree.org — *The Partnership at Drugfree.org*

www.charitywatch.org — *American Institute of Philanthropy*

www.unicefusa.org — *UNICEF*

www.who.int — *World Health Organization*

www.teens.drugabuse.gov — *National Institute for Drug Abuse, NIDA for Teens*